bush
PUBLISHING
& associates

WHAT IS MAN'S
SPIRIT, SOUL & BODY?

Jim Feeley

bush
PUBLISHING
& associates

WHAT IS MAN'S SPIRIT, SOUL & BODY?

ISBN PRINT: 978-1-944566-45-6
ISBN EBOOK: 978-1-944566-46-3
Copyright © 2023 Jim Feeley

Bush Publishing & Associates, LLC books may be ordered everywhere and at Amazon.com.
For further information, please contact:
Bush Publishing & Associates
Tulsa, Oklahoma
www.bushpublishing.com

Printed in the United States of America.

DEDICATION

I want to thank Gail, my wife of 39 years, for her support in writing this book. Throughout my career she has been an anchor that has kept our family together. Much of the success throughout my career is because of the partnership we have established. Our gifts are different but complementary. She has been an anchor for me to maintain our family values and relationships. The writing of this book is no different. While much of the writing has been in the privacy and peacefulness of our home office, she has been very helpful in providing the peace and quietness needed to complete this work.

She has also been the sounding board for me to talk through the ideas and concepts I have written. These talks and discussions have not been seen openly, but this process has helped me to vet many of the ideas that did not make it into this book.

Table of Contents

INTRODUCTION

Do you really know **who** you are? It has been my experience that many people do not have a full perspective of who they are. Or perhaps we should also be asking **what** we are. These are two of the questions that prompted the writing of this book.

Most everyone is consciously aware that they are human beings, and they are aware of their name and the family they come from, and they are aware of their basic characteristics and have a good sense of awareness of how they process their thoughts. We all have some level of awareness of how and why we make our decisions. In most cases, people are generally content with their life decisions.

Presumably, like most people, I have not struggled with my identity. I know who I am, and generally, I have always felt like I know where I'm going. In 1984, as a young man, filled with desire and purpose to be a successful businessman, I reached a point in my life when I realized I needed Divine help in my life. That was when I committed my life to Jesus and was born again. There is no question that this event significantly added to my perspective of purpose in my life.

Not long after my salvation, as a young businessman, I took the time to establish a daily Bible reading plan. I was taught in church that man was a three-part being – spirit, soul, and body but my understanding of what that meant was minimal at best. As I read the Bible and attended church regularly, I gradually gained more spiritual knowledge, and my understanding grew. My Pastor was very good at preaching and teaching the

Word of God. Then in 1995, while on an international trip with my Pastor and brother (also a business partner), I heard a direct word from God to go to Bible school. As an active business owner who saw the challenge of conquering the business world, I was already working long hours to make ends meet. We had already established God as the leader of our business, and consequently, this was not a trivial command for my life nor one that I could ignore. However, with the help and encouragement from my wife and brother and, most importantly, the guidance of the Holy Spirit, I managed to attend Bible school full-time while continuing to work a schedule that most would consider more than full-time. That said, even with the additional education and continued daily Bible reading plan over the decades, I still found scriptures that mentioned the concept of spirit, soul, and body too difficult to understand and effectively process.

Part of the primary challenge is that the soul and spirit are invisible, and they are both immortal. As a born-again believer, I would read the Bible, which said that I was pure, holy, and righteous in God. It was difficult to understand when I knew my thoughts didn't always seem to line up. Who was this referring to?

Consequently, after these decades, I recently committed to studying and understanding the spirit, soul, and body with deeper knowledge and purpose. I began reading and rereading the few books I found on the subject and reviewing dictionaries for a better understanding of these terms, but my understanding still hadn't progressed as I desired. I gained a little more knowledge than before, but it wasn't enough. Then I reread this scripture that I have read and heard many times.

> *Hebrews 4:12 (NKJV) [12] For the word of God is living and powerful, and sharper than any two-edged sword, piercing even to the division of soul and spirit, and of joints and marrow, and is a discerner of the thoughts and intents of the heart.*

INTRODUCTION

This scripture gave me new hope. My summary of this scripture is that the answers I sought are all in the Bible. My interpretation of this scripture is that the Word is so powerful it can discern the difference between the soul and the spirit. I just needed to press into the Word deeper. So, I dove into the scriptures deeper, listened to hours of teaching, read more books, and studied many commentaries. The volume of my notes became overwhelming. At some point, I decided to put my notes into the form of a book to provide some organization of my notes. You are seeing the first compilation of the revelation and illumination of God's Word to me from this study.

Now, as I continue to press in, my eyes have been opened to the scriptures, and I have discovered an abundance of scripture regarding the differences between soul and spirit. I can confidently affirm using the Word of God that man is composed of spirit, soul, and body, and scriptures continue to be revealed to me regarding how God designed us as human beings. We will discuss how He intended us to operate in spirit, soul, and body as one being, just as God designed us to operate.

As an overview, for those of us that are "born-again" we can confidently provide some general statements.

- Our born-again **spirit** is the part of mankind that is God conscious. In other words, we can be consciously aware of Him and maintain an awareness of Him as a Friend, Comforter, Counselor, Savior, and our Life Source. Our spirit is the part of us that was born again when we put our faith in Jesus. And we were given a new spirit (2 Corinthians 5:17). The believer's spirit is the part that has been fully justified, sealed, and redeemed (Ephesians 1:13-14; Romans 8:15-17). It is so pure from sin that the Holy Spirit can and does dwell inside of our spirit so that we can call on Him anytime (John 14:17). The spirit you have now is the same spirit you will have for all eternity, it is perfect (Romans 8; John 14:16).

- The **soul** can be described as your personality, your thoughts, your attitudes and what makes you unique. Perhaps this is why we use words like spirit and soul interchangeably because we cannot see either one, yet we understand that we possess something that makes up who we are as a person. Our soul also incorporates our emotions and our will. Most importantly, we can say our soul is about self-consciousness. We can say that our soul is our central processing system. In our soul, we receive information from our spirit and from our body, and our soul can also produce its own information and opinions. We process this information in our mind and mix it with various emotions and make decisions about what we plan to do.

- Our current **body** is a container for our spirit and the soul while we are on this earth. It is the physical structure of a human. It is our flesh and blood. It is who we are when people look at us. Our body is designed with five senses: seeing, hearing, taste, smell, and touch. All these senses can be used for communicating with the world. Our soul will process this information and determine how we respond.

This is the system God created and established for mankind to operate.

This book reveals biblical, foundational principles with supporting scripture references that will help to understand who and what you are.

- These foundational principles are explained and supported by scriptures.

- All these principles point to Jesus, our true and only Savior.

- Understanding these principles can dramatically change the way you read and understand the Bible.

- Understanding these principles will help you to be victorious in every aspect of your life.

CHAPTER 1

Man is a Created Being

In the beginning, God conceived, created, and established a harmonious universe. God created everything to have its place and function. It was a beautiful, good, and blessed creation. In His creation, God also made special creatures - human beings. Humans represented God in His creation. As part of His design, God created humans as relational beings. Humans were meant to relate to God. He walked and talked with them daily. They were given dominion or authority over the world, and they were the caretakers of the garden. Additionally, they related to each other as God instituted marriage and family life. Let's take a closer look at God's creation.

> *Genesis 1:1 (NKJV)* [1] *In the beginning, God created the heavens and the earth.*

As we study the Bible, we find that God created the heavens for the benefit of the earth. This is no surprise, and it is not difficult to understand this principle. Let's look at just a few of the characteristics of the heavens and the earth. We all know that we receive sunshine, that is, light, from the heavens, and the light from the sunshine releases energy into the life on earth.

Jeremiah 31:35 (NKJV) [35] *Thus says the LORD,*
Who gives the sun for a light by day,
The ordinances of the moon and the stars for a light by night,
Who disturbs the sea,
And its waves roar
(The LORD of hosts is His name):

The light from the sun provides nutrition to plants, animals, and humans. Through the clouds in the sky, which are in the heavens, we get rain, which is fresh, filtered water. Water provides nutrients that are needed to sustain life for plants, animals, and humans. These are both required to sustain life on Earth. Then we can also see that man requires plants and animals to sustain man's life on earth. Plants and trees produce fruits and vegetables for man to eat and sustain his life.

Isaiah 45:18 (NKJV) [18] *For thus says the LORD,*
Who created the heavens,
Who is God,
Who formed the earth and made it,
Who has established it,
Who did not create it in vain,
Who formed it to be inhabited
"I am the LORD, and there is no other".

We see here in Isaiah that God confirmed His purpose in forming the earth was for it to be inhabited. After God created the heavens and the earth, He brought forth life on the earth in the form of grass, herbs, fruit trees, the birds of the air, the fish in the sea and the creatures of the earth. After He created all of these, then He created man. So, we can see God created the heavens for the earth, the earth for man, and man is for God.

We see that there was a proper order to God's creation with the heavens serving the life on earth, the life on earth serving man and man serving

God, who is life. Now let's take a much closer look at the creation of mankind.

> *Genesis 1:26-28 (NKJV) Then God said, "Let Us make man in Our image, according to Our likeness; let them have dominion over the fish of the sea, over the birds of the air, and over the cattle, over all the earth and over every creeping thing that creeps on the earth." ²⁷ So **God created man in His own image**; in the image of God He created him; male and female He created them. ²⁸ Then God blessed them, and God said to them, "Be fruitful and multiply; fill the earth and subdue it; **have dominion** over the fish of the sea, over the birds of the air, and over every living thing that moves on the earth."*

There are many things we can learn from these three verses. However, let us focus on three key elements.

1. God created mankind.
2. Mankind was created in the image and likeness of God.
3. Mankind was created to subdue the earth and have dominion or rule the earth.

Man was Created by God

The first thing God said in verse 26 was "Let Us **make** man". Scripture is very clear that we did not evolve, and we are not related to monkeys or apes. We did not just magically appear out of nowhere as some theories suggest. Many people throughout history have attempted to distort this scripture with made up stories or theories about the origin of mankind. This scripture plainly says, "Let Us **make** man". Genesis 2:7 says He formed us. Can you imagine watching God in the process of forming mankind with His hands? Did He use any tools or equipment? Did He have a workshop?

Let's take some time to ponder the process of God creating mankind. Try and picture God forming the body of man from the dust of the ground. It is much more involved than molding a blob of clay or mud into a statue in the shape of a man, and then breathing into man's nostrils and magically man has a spirit, soul, and body, each with a tremendous amount of complex detail that just happened to come together.

While we do not have all the details of His creation process, we do know it involved much more than our outward shape. God had to design and assemble each of our organs and members in a manner that allows us to function, to sustain life, and reproduce. It is easy to overlook the complexity of this process. How does the heart fit near the lungs and why is it near the lungs? Why do we need a pancreas or liver? How do our lungs act as a filter and how much air/oxygen do we require? Why do we require oxygen? Why do we need blood and what is blood made of? How does the heart regulate the flow of blood? Which minerals were required to form each organ? What is the proper mixture of each mineral? These are just a few very high-level questions that can seem overwhelming. Mankind has been studying the design and function of our body since the beginning of time and we still have many unanswered questions. However, man can answer some of these questions now as a post creation analysis, but remember God started with a blank page and the dust of the earth. Mankind is studying what is in existence whereas God started with His own idea.

> *Zechariah 12:1 says that God stretched forth the heavens, laid the foundation of the earth, and **formed the spirit of man**.*

So, this verse confirms that God also formed our spirit. In this book, we will also be asking and answering many questions about the design and function of our soul and spirit. We can easily acknowledge characteristics of our bodies, but what does the Bible tell us about the characteristics of our soul and spirit?

In Our Image and Likeness

Genesis 1:26 (NKJV) Then God said, "Let Us make man in Our image, according to Our likeness;" ...

Who is God referring to when He said let "*Us*" make man? The actual Hebrew name for God used here is Elohim. It is in the plural and refers to the Father, Son, and Holy Spirit. It has a broad perspective but generally speaks of His greatness, and His might.

We are made in Their image according to Their likeness. A key point we learn from this verse is that we are not God, but we are made in Their image and according to Their likeness.

We should recognize the importance of this statement. No other creature was designed in Their image and likeness, so we should be recognizing the privilege and importance that God has for mankind. Our whole being is designed in the image and likeness of God. He has a spirit, soul, and body. Likewise, man also has a spirit, soul, and body. *"In His image and likeness"*. But what does this mean? How can we define or understand this statement? Let's start with the question: what is the difference between image and likeness? The fact that these two words are used separately in the same sentence would generally imply that they have different meanings. However, from my study it appears many Bible scholars agree that these two words carry a similar meaning. I have not found solid information to dispute that opinion, however it does appear to me that there are two aspects of these words that we can capture through the scriptures. That is that they involve both character and functions.

Let's look at some other scriptures using these words.

> *Genesis 5:3 (NKJV)* ³ *And Adam lived one hundred and thirty years, and begat a son in **his own likeness, after his image**, and named him Seth.*

It is interesting that the bible uses the same words for Seth but not any other direct children of Adam. The words likeness and image are also reversed. Does this mean that Seth looked more like Adam, or he thinks and processes more like Adam, or his character simulates Adam's character?

> *Genesis 4:25-26 (NKJV) And Adam knew his wife again, and she bore a son and named him Seth, "For God has appointed another seed for me instead of Abel, whom Cain killed."* ²⁶ *And as for Seth, to him also a son was born; and he named him Enosh. Then men began to call on the name of the LORD.*

This scripture is a key to the answer – Seth was the next in line to carry the Seed. It would have been Able who called on the name of God, but he was killed by Cain who rejected God. Seth then became the father of Enosh, and we can continue to trace the genealogy in the Bible from Adam, through Seth and Enosh all the way to King David and further to Mary who gave birth to Jesus our Savior. So, Seth was appointed by God to be another seed instead of Able to carry and transfer the Seed of our Savior Jesus Christ. When this scripture says "*then men began to call on the name of the Lord*" it is referring to the character of a person. In other words, Seth and Enosh were effective leaders that continued to guide men to call on the name of the Lord. We will expand on this perspective on genealogy later.

Characteristics of God

As we consider the character of God the first and most important thing to recognize is that God is the very essence of love. Whenever we look to God, we can see His love at the center of His actions. Recognizing and remembering this attribute in every aspect of our lives might be the most important and valuable thing in our lives!

Now let's consider a sampling of scriptures that focus on other characteristics of God that specifically relate to man being the image and likeness of God.

> *Genesis 9:5-6 (NKJV) Surely for your lifeblood I will demand a reckoning; from the hand of every beast I will require it, and from the hand of man. From the hand of every man's brother I will require the life of man.*
> *6 "Whoever sheds man's blood,"*
> *By man his blood shall be shed;*
> *For in **the image of God***
> *He made man.*

This scripture is simply saying that because man is made in the image of God, his life is worthy of honor and respect and whoever kills a man will be held accountable. The next scripture is similar.

> *James 3:9 (NIV) 9 With the tongue we praise our Lord and Father, and with it we curse human beings, who have been **made in God's likeness**.*

James is talking about taming the tongue or watching the words we speak. Again, the reference is to honor and respect not only to our Lord and Father but also to other human beings, because we are made in God's likeness.

Ephesians 4:24 (NIV) [24] *and to put on the new self, created* **to be like God** *in true righteousness and holiness.*

We are created to be like God in true righteousness and holiness. This again refers to man's character or new nature. This scripture is specifically referring to the regenerated man or born-again person that is a new creation in Christ.

Colossians 3:10 (NIV) 10 and have put on the new self, which is being renewed in knowledge **in the image of its Creator.**

This scripture refers to the born-again believer who is renewing his soul in knowledge in the image of its Creator. This is talking about forgetting our old sinful self or sinful nature and walking in our new, born-again nature which is in the image of our Creator. It goes on to describe this new nature as holy, compassionate, kind, humble, gentle, and patient.

1 John 3:2-5 (NIV) Dear friends, now we are children of God, and what we will be has not yet been made known. But we know that when Christ appears, **we shall be like him,** *for we shall see him as he is.* [3] *All who have this hope in him purify themselves, just as he is pure.* [4] *Everyone who sins breaks the law; in fact, sin is lawlessness.* [5] *But you know that he appeared so that he might take away our sins. And in him is no sin.*

Here is another scripture that says we shall be like Him. This is again referring to the born-again believer and is referring to purification of ourselves. Jesus came to take away our sins so that we could return to the status that He originally designed in Adam, and we can be without sin. When He takes away our sins we are like God.

Colossians 1:15-16 (NIV) **The Son is the image of the invisible God,** *the firstborn over all creation.* [16] *For in him all things were created: things in heaven and on earth, visible and invisible, whether thrones or powers or rulers or authorities; all things have been created through him and for him.*

The Son is referring to Jesus Christ as a man and He also came into this world in the image of God. In this scripture we also learn God is invisible. No surprises as everyone understands that. But it goes on to speak of Jesus Christ's authority over all creation. God the Father is the ruler over everything. As a member of the Trinity, Jesus Christ rules with Him. The Son of God left His throne in heaven to become a man, but still in the image of God just like us. He gave His life for us and became the firstborn over death, meaning He conquered death and took back the authority Adam gave up. The conclusion we should recognize is that regardless of the circumstances Jesus Christ is a conqueror and ruler, and we are made in His image and likeness!

*2 Corinthians 4:4-6 (NIV) The god of this age has blinded the minds of unbelievers, so that they cannot see the light of the gospel that displays the glory of Christ, who **is the image of God**. [5] For what we preach is not ourselves, but Jesus Christ as Lord, and ourselves as your servants for Jesus' sake. [6] For God, who said, "Let light shine out of darkness," made his light shine in our hearts to give us the light of the knowledge of God's glory displayed in the face of Christ.*

Here we learn that Christ, who is the image of God, is the light of the good news that displays the glory of Jesus Christ. Just as during the creation process God the Father said *"Let light come out of darkness"* Jesus Christ let His light shine in our hearts so that His glory can be revealed in us and through us.

To summarize, we have just reviewed several scriptures (and there are many more that could have been added) that reveal what God meant when He said, *"let Us make man in Our image according to Our likeness"*. We can see that the words image and likeness do not point to physical similarities. These scriptures refer more to the moral and spiritual similarities of God's character.

The image and likeness of God is the expression of who God is in all His attributes and virtues. This image is not the physical form, because all of God's attributes and virtues are invisible. These are the characteristics of God. He is full of invisible attributes and virtues. Christ is the expression of all that God is in His attributes and virtues, and this expression is the image and likeness thereof. Thus, the image and likeness of God is the expression of God in all that He is. We could also say characteristics and qualities.

Image is not referring to a molded figure that can be worshiped, but it is the very expression of who or what God is. This means that God made man to have the attributes and virtues that He has. When God created man, He created him in His image and likeness, according to His attributes and virtues, so that man can express God through these attributes and virtues. For example, God has love, and God loves. God also created man that man may have love and that man may love. God has wisdom and God has His purpose, so God made man also to have wisdom and to have a purpose.

While there are many attributes to express the character of God, perhaps the most important characteristic that stands out is love. To know and understand God is to know and understand love. This is not intended to diminish the value of other attributes of God, rather it is intended to enhance His other attributes. Love is always at the root of all Godly principles.

Functions of God

There are also many functions of God. God can think, God can consider, God can love, God can like and dislike, God can make choices, God can have intentions, and God can make decisions. God created man in the same way so that man could express God. What man has, however, is only the image of God's attributes and virtues but not the reality. So, let's look at some of the functions of God that are expressed in man.

Another perspective of His image and likeness could be that God created us as a three-part being with spirit, soul, and body just like God has a Spirit, Soul, and Body. We see that God appeared to Abraham in Genesis 18 in the likeness of a man. He appeared to Abraham in a visible way with man's likeness. Man's image and likeness is after God's image and likeness. We human beings have a physical body; God has a spiritual body. We also have our inner being (spirit and soul). In the same way, God has His inner being. Man's outward body was created after the image and likeness of God. Before God was incarnated to be a man (referring to Jesus), He appeared to Abraham in the form of a man. The form of man is the form of God, for man was created after the image and likeness of God.

God has a Spirit –

> *Genesis 1:2 (NKJV) ² The earth was without form, and void; and darkness was on the face of the deep. And the* **Spirit of God** *was hovering over the face of the waters.*

God has a soul –

> *Jeremiah 32:41 (NKJV) ⁴¹ Yes, I will rejoice over them to do them good, and I will assuredly plant them in this land, with all* **My heart and with all My soul.'**

In this verse God tells us directly that He has a heart and soul. If we just look at the creation itself, it is easy to see that God has a mind and imagination that is beyond our comprehension. His emotions are vivid. Emotions of love, joy, anger, gladness, and other emotions that we find in ourselves. God has a will. Mathew 6:10 "Y*our **will** be done on earth as it is in heaven*".

God the Father has a body –

Numerous scriptures throughout the Bible identify parts of God's body. We know God has hands because Genesis 2:7 says He formed Adam with His hands. God has feet; Genesis 3:8 says the man and his wife heard the sound of the Lord walking in the garden. God has eyes; 2 Chronicles 16:9 says the eyes of the Lord run to and fro throughout the earth. God has a face; Exodus 33:11 says The Lord would speak to Moses face-to-face as one would speak to a friend. God has fingers; Exodus 31:18 says ...and He gave him the two tablets of the covenant of law, the tablets of stone inscribed by the finger of God. We can go on as the scriptures show us that He has a voice to speak, ears to hear, arms, legs, and back.

> *Hebrews 1:3 (NIV) **The Son is the radiance of God's glory and the exact representation of his being**, sustaining all things by his powerful word. After he had provided purification for sins, he sat down at the right hand of the Majesty in heaven.*

"The Son is the radiance of God's glory" is speaking about Jesus Christ, …. "the exact representation of His being" … which is referring to His Father. We also know that as the Son of God, He humbled Himself as He left His throne in heaven and came to earth to be born as a man with a physical body just like ours. Prior to His physical birth on earth, Jesus Christ always existed but in divine spiritual status, not as a physical being with flesh and blood. He was born in the flesh as a man to be a

sacrifice for us. This scripture refers to His resurrected status in heaven in His spiritual status.

> *Titus 1:1-3 (NKJV)* [1] *Paul, a bondservant of God and an apostle of Jesus Christ, according to the faith of God's elect and the acknowledgment of the truth which accords with godliness,* [2] *in hope of* **eternal life** *which God, who cannot lie, promised before time began,* [3] *but has in due time manifested His word through preaching, which was committed to me according to the commandment of God our Savior;*

We also know that God's body is eternal. He is, always was, and always will be. Adam's body was created in the **image and likeness** of God and Adam was designed to last forever even though Adam was created with a physical body not a spiritual body. God made Adam's body from elements of the earth. We see in these opening verses in Titus that before time began it was God's plan that man shall live with Him in eternity.

> *1 Corinthians 15:45-49 (NKJV) And so it is written, "The first man Adam became a living being." The last Adam became a life-giving spirit.*[46] *However, the spiritual is not first, but the natural, and afterward the spiritual.* [47] *The first man was of the earth, made of dust; the second Man is the Lord from heaven.* [48] *As was the man of dust, so also are those who are made of dust; and as is the heavenly Man, so also are those who are heavenly.* [49] *And as we have borne the* **image and likeness** *of the man of dust, we shall also bear the* **image and likeness** *of the heavenly Man.*

We know from Genesis that the first Adam was made in His image and likeness. His body was made of natural resources, and he became a human being. The first Adam changed the functions of his being when he sinned. This scripture therefore is defining the fallen Adam as a natural man or his flesh. As descendants of the fallen Adam, we are also fleshly or natural men, and we were born in Adam's image and likeness. That is, until the last Adam and as a regenerated man our spirit bears the image and likeness of Jesus Christ.

The Father, the Son, and the Holy Spirit

God is three persons in one. They operate in perfect unison as if they are one but they each have unique roles, responsibilities, and personalities. We are introduced to Them in the first verse of the Bible.

> *Genesis 1:1 (NKJV)* [1] *In the beginning God created the heavens and the earth.*

The word used for God in this scripture is Elohim. It is a plural word that refers to the oneness of God. In other words, it refers to the Holy Trinity – God the Father, God the Son, and God the Holy Spirit, as one God.

> *Genesis 1:26 (NKJV)* [26] *Then God said, "Let Us make man in Our **image**, according to Our **likeness**; let them have dominion over the fish of the sea, over the birds of the air, and over the cattle, over all the earth and over every creeping thing that creeps on the earth."*

Notice that God said – "let Us". He is referring to the Trinity. They are all three involved in the creation process.

> *Genesis 2:7 (NKJV)* [7] *And the LORD God formed man of the dust of the ground, and breathed into his nostrils the breath of life; and man became a living being.*

The breath of life is referring to the Holy Spirit who gave the power to man.

- **God the Father**
  - o   He is the Architect, and He is Head of Operations.
  - o   He said, "let there be light",
  - o   He brings the ideas - to create the earth and man, to save humanity, to send His Son.
- **God the Son**
  - o   He is the Builder and Administrator
  - o   He is the doer of operations, Jesus said, I came to do the will of my Father.
  - o   Jesus Christ is the will of God in action.
- **God the Spirit**
  - o   He manifests the actions or operations and doing in our lives.
  - o   He is the Power.
  - o   He is the revealer.

God the Father says, "let there be light." God the Son "turns the light switch on", and God the Spirit who brings the power. He is the "generator or power" of the Trinity. He is also the power in our life.

God the Father so loved the world that **He sent** His Son. It was His Son, Jesus who came and died on the cross. Jesus did the will of His Father. He is the doer. It was the Holy Spirit who brought salvation into our hearts. Without the Holy Spirit there would be no faith in our heart, it would just be a story. The Holy Spirit brings us revelation. Christianity is a revelation, and the Holy Spirit is the revealer of Jesus Christ in a believer's life. The Holy Spirit is the first manifestation in our life. Without Him we wouldn't know how to come to the Lord. He brings conviction, He brings us to the cross and begins regeneration – the new birth. He then sanctifies and sets us apart. Adam came alive when the breath of God (Holy Spirit) entered his fleshly body. The church was born (came alive) when the Holy Spirit came upon the 120 in the upper room on the day of Pentecost. Jesus told them to wait in Jerusalem until the Holy Spirit comes because He knew they needed the power and comfort of the Holy Spirit.

> *Psalms 33:6 (NKJV) ⁶ By the word of the LORD the heavens were made, And all the host of them by the breath of His mouth.*

This scripture is talking about God's creation. The heavens are referring to the atmosphere around the earth where the clouds, stars and planets are located. The host of them is likely referring to Genesis 2:1 which is speaking of all the newly created inhabitants of the heavens and the earth such as birds and all the living creatures that had the breath of God.

John chapter 1 tells us that Jesus is the Word of God. We see here in Psalms 33:6 that by the **Word** of Yahweh (or Jesus Christ) the heavens were made, He is the Builder. And the host of them by the **Breath** of His mouth. It is the Breath of the Holy Spirit that gave life to all the creatures on earth. They, referring to Elohim, worked individually, but together in the creation process.

In the natural, breath comes from our lungs and moves air through our vocal cords which gives us the power to speak as we form our mouth and tongue in a manner to form specific sounds and words. So, breath is required for us to speak. Breath is the **power** that is needed to speak. This breath or power is like the Holy Spirit. So, the Word without the Breath would not reach us – it is the power of the Breath that releases the Word to us. In other words, creation required teamwork of the Godhead, who is Elohim.

> *Ezekiel 36:27 (NKJV) ²⁷ I will put My Spirit within you and cause you to walk in My statutes, and you will keep My judgments and do them.*

The Holy Spirit helps us obey God.

> *1 Peter 1:2 (NKJV)* [2] *elect according to **the foreknowledge** **of God the Father,** in **sanctification of the Spirit,** for* **obedience and sprinkling of the blood of Jesus Christ:** *Grace to you and peace be multiplied.*

Again, we see the Trinity here. The **"foreknowledge of God the Father"** – He is the planner. Then we see the **Spirit sanctifies us** and it is the Spirit who is the one who sprinkles the **blood of Jesus to help us in obedience.** And it was God the Son who provided the blood.

So, these functions of God help us in understanding the Trinity. They are three persons in one. They have different roles, but they are always in perfect unison. They created us as a spirit, soul, and body. We also should operate in unison because we were made in Their image and likeness.

Man is Spirit, Soul, and Body

Our human "being"consists of three-parts – spirit, soul, and body. Many experts including psychologists, scientists, medical experts, and even some Bible scholars believe that man is a body with a soul – a two part being. In fact, many of them recognize that our body is the fleshy part of our being and man's soul is invisible and nonmaterial separate from the fleshy part of our bodies. Others believe the soul is part of the brain which is an organ in the body which makes us only a body. God's Word however makes it clear that we also have a spirit, so we are a three-part being. There is structure and organization to man's profile as a three-part being.

As the Apostle Paul is praying for the Thessalonians, he specifically draws attention to the whole man – spirit, soul, and body.

1 Thessalonians 5:23 (NKJV) [23] *Now may the God of peace Himself sanctify you completely; and may your whole **spirit, soul, and body** be preserved blameless at the coming of our Lord Jesus Christ.*

Paul recognizes that all three-parts are separate, but we are still one person. And he is praying for each part because he understands that all three-parts need God's help. We will use the Word of God to not only establish that we are spirit, soul, and body and we will use the Word to separate these parts of man to help us better understand ourselves.

Hebrews 4:12 (NKJV) [12] *For the word of God is living and powerful, and sharper than any two-edged sword, piercing even to the division of soul and spirit, and of joints and marrow, and is a discerner of the thoughts and intents of the heart.*

The author of Hebrews tells us that man's soul and spirit are so tightly knit together that only the Word of God is sharper than any double-edged sword and can divide the soul and spirit. Let's take a closer look at the two analogies that are shown, beginning with the first metaphor of *"joints and marrow."*

1. This scripture is comparing our **soul to a joint**. A joint is a connector and connects two things together. In this case our soul is the connector between our spirit and body, therefore our soul is linking all three together as one person – spirit, soul, and body.

2. Next is a comparison of **marrow to our spirit**. Marrow is in the center of our bones, and it produces blood cells. Life is in the blood and blood circulates throughout our body giving it life. Similarly, our spirit is the center or core of our being and receives life from God and provides life throughout our being and cleansing our souls from sin.

3. A further perspective in comparing marrow to our spirit is that marrow is in the center of the bone. It is a soft fatty substance that produces blood cells. Marrow is recognized as a nourishment and strengthener to the bones. So, while it is deep on the inside of man it releases strength to the outward man which is the soul. They are somewhat blended together but still separate.

This scripture provides tremendous insight to understanding how God created mankind. Now let's briefly consider the second analogy of *"and is a discerner of the thoughts and intents of the heart."*

1. Our soul is the ***"discerner of the thoughts."*** Thoughts can come from a variety of sources and are processed in our soul. We "choose" or "will" what we desire to do with each thought. We can dwell on any thought, or we can ignore or take our thoughts captive. In other words, thoughts are like seeds (good or bad), that can grow and develop fruit, or they can be destroyed depending on how we reasoned that thought in our mind and what we chose to do with that thought.

2. ***"Intents of our heart"*** come when you dwell on a thought then allow that thought to be deposited into our heart, and it becomes our intention or something we desire to further develop. In other words, not every thought becomes an intent.

It is only the Word of God that can help us to discern these differences. This scripture is a key reference that will help guide our study in discerning the unique characteristics of our spirit, soul, and body and God's perfect design of how our total being works together as one.

If scientists and other experts do not use the Word of God to understand man, they will never be able to understand that at man's core is his spirit.

We will review how all three-parts of our being work together to bring righteousness, peace, and joy into man's life so that we can have a relationship with the God who created us and loves us. Usually when you buy a piece of machinery, equipment or even a toy it comes with an operator's manual. Many of us tend to open the box and begin the assembly process before reading the directions. Then after we get part of the assembly completed, we realize that we missed a step and need to disassemble and start over after we read the instructions. In this case the Bible is our operator's manual that will identify the parts of mankind, it will show us how we operate, it includes a repair manual, and it will include maintenance schedules.

God created us with all three of the dimensions that make up our profile and they are designed to work together. Each part of us has its own purpose and function.

- Man through his **body** communicates with the outward world through his five senses: sight, hearing, touch, smell, and taste. His body is worldly conscious.

- Man through his **soul** can know himself through three primary functions; mind, will, and emotions. His soul is what we call self-conscious and is a connector of body and spirit.

- Man through his **spirit** has the capacity to know God through three primary functions: communion, intuition, and conscience. His spirit is conscious of spiritual matters and specifically is designed to have the capacity to be God conscious.

Man was Made to Rule

The third point to recognize is that He made man to rule over the fish in the sea and the birds in the sky, over the livestock and all the wild animals, and over all the creatures that move along the ground.

Simply put man was created to rule the earth. The earth was made for mankind.

> *Genesis 1:26 (NIV)* [26] *Then God said, "Let us make mankind in our image, in our likeness, **so that** they may **rule** over the fish in the sea and the birds in the sky, over the livestock and all the wild animals, and over all the creatures that move along the ground."*

One reason the Bible states that we were made in Their image and likeness is to **rule** over His creation. This was a privilege and a responsibility that was only given to mankind. It doesn't say that He gave authority to the angels to rule the earth. It says, They (Elohim) created mankind to rule the earth.

It is clear in Genesis chapter 1 that God created the earth and everything in it. As such He obviously owns the earth and everything that is in it.

> *Psalms 24:1 (NKJV)* [1] *The earth is the LORD's, and all its fullness, The world and those who dwell therein.*

This scripture is only one of many that validate His ownership in writing. As the creator and possessor, God can do as He chooses with the world. In Genesis 1:26 He said that They made mankind so that they may rule over His creation. God is still the owner, but He created mankind so that he could be the manager or ruler over the world because God created a world of order. He created a world with order, with foundations and structure, precept upon precept, and He included authority in His design. As the owner He put Adam (mankind) man in authority.

To put this in terms that we commonly use, we could say that God is the owner of the world, and He gave mankind a lease to manage the world. This lease would have covered management of everything in and on the earth. That means every living thing, animals of every kind, from larger beasts to the smallest of insects. The sea and every fish in it including the smallest living organism in the sea. It would also include the birds and the atmosphere that they fly in. In other words, everything in the realm of the world was covered under this lease.

So, we can say that the very structure of mankind, (spirit, soul, body) was designed to rule the world that God created. Man was intended to fellowship and to be in intimate communication with God by his spirit and to receive guidance, understanding, and the love of God through his spirit. This is a key point to understand.

God created man to receive life through his spirit because that is the method that God chose to communicate with man. All the life resources or directions that Adam would receive from God would flow through his spirit and into his soul. [Diagram 1]

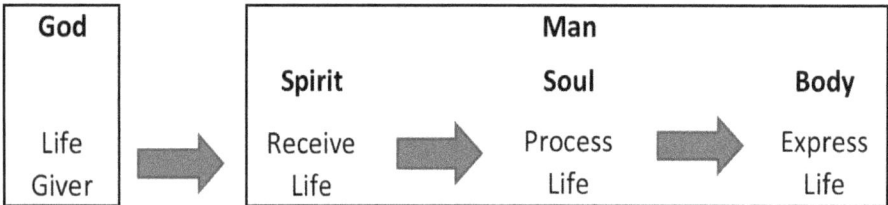

God	Man		
	Spirit	**Soul**	**Body**
Life Giver	Receive Life	Process Life	Express Life

The life resources from God were to be **received** in man's spirit and **processed** in his soul. In his soul he could process the goodness from God through his reasoning and incorporate his emotions with the intent to align his will with God's will. He could then **express** this same life that he received from God through his fleshly body into the world. This is the manner that God designed the flow of life through man's being to effectively rule the earth according to His design.

What was involved in Adam's position as ruler? What were his responsibilities? Since there was no sin on/in the earth it is difficult to fully recognize what was required of Adam. Generally speaking, as a ruler he would be required to be the leader that can develop structures of organization, planning programs that provide for the love and care for everything including every creature that is on earth. That would include being a protector against predators. However, the only potential predator at this time was Satan and his minions. Demons didn't have direct access to the world, but as we know, Satan still figured out how to sneak in the back door.

> God designed man's spirit, soul, and body in such a manner that he could be an effective ruler of the world.

Mankind would also be the organizer of the natural needs including food sources for mankind and all of the plants and creatures on earth and in the sea. For example, as the animal kingdom grew perhaps the garden needed to be expanded, which meant more tilling, sowing and maintenance. These are just a few observations but remember this includes everything on earth. It was a big job. God gave Adam everything he needed to rule effectively.

To summarize, all three of these points that were established in verse 26 –

1. *"Let Us make mankind"*

2. *......in Our image, in Our likeness,*

3. *"....so that they may rule......".*

Then the Word confirms the importance of these three points as they are immediately repeated in verse 27, 28. However, in verse 27 the Word adds clarity and says, God created mankind and then continues to say that He created them male and female, so he also created woman. Note that there are two and only two genders in mankind. And God established which was male and which was female. There was not any confusion about gender. It is not the role of human beings to re-appoint a man as a woman or vice-versa or some new gender.

Then in verse 28 He blessed them and said be fruitful and increase in number. To increase in number or multiply is simple and straightforward but when adding fruitful it adds a dimension of quantity and quality and it is a good quality. Fruit is the product of sowing seed.

Also, in verse 28 God repeats, *"fill the earth and subdue it (or bring it into subjection)"*. Then one more time He states, "**Rule** *over the fish in the sea and the birds in the sky and over every living creature that moves on the ground."* God clearly wants us to know what He expects us to do and understand our role on this planet (*to rule*).

CHAPTER 2

Introduction to the First Adam

As we open this chapter let's start with Adam's name. God named his first created human being Adam. In Hebrew the word Adam can refer to an individual's name or it can refer to a general noun, meaning mankind as it represents all of humanity. Therefore, Adam is an appropriate name since he was the first person that was created and brought into existence. As such, many times throughout this book we will utilize his name accordingly. We will also refer to man or mankind in general terms to include both male and female. In the Old Testament alone the noun Adam (mankind) is used over five hundred times. Additionally in the New Testament Adam is sometimes referred to as the first Adam. Specifically in these instances he is referred to as the representative of mankind, or the original example of what every person born thereafter will resemble, in terms of image and likeness. We could also say Adam's DNA represents the nature of mankind in structure and character.

How Did God Create Adam?

What are the life elements of the spirit, soul, and body of mankind? How are they assembled and how do they work together? Let us open the operator's manual and start by looking closely at God's creation.

*Genesis 2:7 (CWSB) ⁷ And the LORD God formed man of the dust of the ground and **breathed** into his nostrils the **breath of life**; and man became a **living soul**.*

We see in this scripture that God started creating Adam's body first by forming it from the dust of the ground. As we already discussed there is not much detail about the forming process of Adam's body mentioned in scripture. We do obtain various details throughout the Bible that references elements of man's body such as bone, marrow, ligaments, blood, various organs, and others. We will discuss more details about the body and flesh later, but the important thing to recognize at this point is that the body on its own does not have life, because this was only the

> *Adam's body was lifeless, it came to life when he received the "breath of life."*

first step in creating Adam. Adam's body did not show any signs of life or come alive until God finished the next step when God gave Adam his spirit and soul.

Then, after God formed the body or flesh of Adam, God breathed the *"breath of life"* into Adam's body. When He did that, man became a living soul, meaning that Adam's body had received the breath of life, which then made him alive (a living soul) and his newly created life also included a spirit. Now the creation of Adam was complete, and his body was fully functioning. Adam was able to breathe air into his lungs, his heart pumped blood throughout his body, he could hear and see and do all the physical things God designed for him to do. We also know that Adam's spirit and soul were also fully functioning because life flowed throughout his being.

The Hebrew word for breath in *"**breath** of life"* in this verse is neshamah, Strong's #5397, meaning breath, wind, spirit. The meaning of breath or neshamah can be broad, and it is used in various translations as breath, wind, or spirit. For example,

> *Proverbs 20:27 (NKJV)* [27] *The spirit of a man is the lamp of the LORD, Searching all the inner depths of his heart.*

Here in Proverbs, we see the word "spirit" is Strong's #5397- neshamah, which is the same word used for "breath". Now if we go back to Gen. 2:7 it says when God breathed the "breath of life" into Adam he became a "living soul". The Hebrew word for *"living **soul**",* is nephesh, Strong's # 5315, meaning breath, the inner being with its thoughts, will, and emotions. This refers to the soul and can include man and animals in that description. The *"**soul**"* brings breath to all creatures and man, which brings life and animation to the body or flesh. Nephesh is what animates the body and brings life to our physical body. Breath is required for man or creatures (animals) to continue life in a physical body, but only man has a spirit. So, we conclude that the *"breath of life"* into Adam included his soul and his spirit.

Let's consider what God included in His creation of all the creatures.

> *Genesis 7:15 (NKJV) And they went into the ark to Noah, two by two, **of all flesh in which is the breath of life.***

We can see in this scripture that all flesh meaning every creature on earth came to life by the *"breath of life"*. In other words, every creature including insects, birds, and animals have a soul and their soul was imparted into them as the breath of life which is from the Holy Spirit. In this verse the word breath in "**breath** of life" is translated from the Hebrew word "ruwach" which is Strong's # 7307, which can also be translated as breath, wind, spirit, or mind. So, the *"breath of life"* that is breathed into animals is a different word than that used for the "breath of life" in Adam but can be translated in a similar manner. No other scriptures suggest that any other creatures have a spirit, they only have a body and a soul. So, we can conclude that in this instance "ruwach" is referring to the mind or soul.

Occasionally, when scripture uses nephesh in reference to man it incorporates the whole man - spirit, soul, and body, but generally it is more restricted to the soulish realm. Gen 2:7 says God breathed the **breath of life** into Adam's nostrils. So, God breathed the neshamah or spirit or breath of life and the man became a living soul or being. This is like the same process of all creatures; however we also know that mankind was created in His image and His likeness and therefore we can conclude Genesis 2:7 was how and when God imparted spirit and soul into the body of Adam (mankind).

All other creatures on earth were different. A primary distinction between man and animals is that we as humans have a spirit just like God, who is Spirit, thus making man a three-part being and animals two part being.

What is Life?

While many words that are translated from Hebrew to English such as, life or living, they often share the same or similar root words, in Hebrew they frequently use variations and morphology including tense, plurality, and gender that can alter the final meaning. Many times, these variations and morphology are not distinguished in Bible translations from Hebrew to English. Additionally, sometimes we must search for other scriptures to understand and confirm our understanding. This is the case here for the words we have been reviewing: breath, life, living, soul, and spirit.

Our society would generally acknowledge that life would be recognized when something is growing, loving, breathing, moving, or thinking. These are all attributes of life, but far from being all inclusive.

In Genesis 2:7 we reviewed the first part of "*Breath of life*." Now let's take a closer look at the next part of Breath of **Life**. This word **life** in Hebrew is "*chay*", Strong's #2416 means alive or life. The same root word is used for animals, birds, plants, and man. Additionally, this same root of this word is also used to describe "**living** soul" when describing the completed man. The same root word is used to describe "**living** creature" when describing all the creatures other than man. And finally, this same root word chay can even be used to describe life in plants and trees.

However, as life is used in Genesis 2:7 it specifically refers to the life of mankind as a whole, including his spirit, soul, and body. Let's breakdown a view of life in each part of man's being. To help understand life we can focus our attention on the source of life.

Body

As we just mentioned, in the Old Testament the Hebrew word for physical life is chay and in the New Testament is the Greek word bios. Both words are most commonly used to refer to physical life, or life in the flesh, or life in this world and this physical life or flesh.

> *Chay, bios, physical are the same word in different languages. They all refer to worldly or physical life.*

Chay, bios or physical life can be summed up as life that relates to the world. Without this part or form of life we can't relate to anyone or anything in this physical world on earth. It also has a close relationship with the soul. Particularly it frequently relates to flesh as a fleshy part of man's life. When God created man's body it was flesh. There was not any life in his body until the Holy Spirit breathed the breath of life (neshamah) into him. It was his spirit and soul that God breathed into Adam and brought life into Adam's body and gave it the ability to function or in other words gave his body or flesh animation. This animation releases man's five senses and allows them to operate on earth. We know these senses as seeing, hearing, tasting, smelling, and feeling. It is through the animation of these five senses that mankind can relate with the world.

So, without the soul neither mankind nor animals can experience life on earth. In our society today medical and legal experts define death as the *"irreversible cessation of cardiorespiratory function or irreversible cessation of all brain function."* In simple terms if our heart stops pumping blood throughout our body and our brain stops telling our body to breathe then our body is considered dead.

It is man's and animal's soul that is the direct source of life that brings animation of those functions to sustain life in the physical body.

> *The soul brings animation or life to the physical body*

Soul

The Hebrew word for soul is **nephesh** and the Greek word for soul is **psuche**. Usually, these words for soul are used in the Bible to reference only the soul or in other words they can refer to **soulish life**. However, it is worth noting that occasionally they are used to refer to man's life as a composite whole.

The soul is where we obtain awareness of life or self-consciousness. Three primary components of our soul are our intellect, emotions, and our will. In other words, it is where we think, feel, and choose. Man's soul is a required element to provide life and animation to his body. His soul will tell his body how and when to breathe, and how every bodily function is to operate. His soul cannot facilitate anything on earth without his body, and his body cannot operate without his soul. The same is true for every earthly creature that God created. They all have a soul and live in a physical body. When a man's soul departs from his body then his body dies and returns to dust. So, his soul provides life to his body.

The soul is generally used to describe "you." It is who you are, your consciousness. It is your personality. Your soul obtains awareness of the physical world through your body. Your soul also obtains awareness of the spiritual world through your spirit. In other words, your soul is you or your own world. It allows you to be aware of the physical world through your body and the spiritual world through your spirit, and it makes you aware of yourself.

When God created Adam (mankind) He designed man's soul to receive life from his spirit. However, we will see how that has changed throughout history.

Spirit

Man also has a spirit. Man is the only physical being (flesh and blood) that has a spirit. That is because God is Spirit and God relates with man through man's spirit. God created man in His own likeness and image. Man is special to God and has been given benefits, privileges, and responsibilities above all creatures on earth. A key benefit is that we have a spirit. When God created Adam (mankind), He designed a flow of life in him. All life begins with God.

> *John 6:63 (NKJV)* ⁶³ *It is the Spirit who gives life; the flesh profits nothing. The words that I speak to you are spirit, and they are life.*

When God speaks, His Words are spirit and life. This scripture makes understanding this concept simple because it says the source of man's life is the Spirit of God. Since God created everything including man, this statement seems obvious. But we are referring here to the flow of life. It starts with God who is life, and He communicates life to us through His words which are spirit and life.

> John 10:10 (NKJV) ¹⁰ *The thief does not come except to steal, and to kill, and to destroy. I have come that they may have **life**, and that they may have it more abundantly.*

The word **life** as highlighted in this scripture is the Greek word **zoe**. It infers spiritual life that can flow throughout man's being. As such when God speaks into man's spirit, He is speaking zoe life into man's spirit. God's design of man's being is that man receives zoe life when God speaks into his spirit, and then that life from God should flow from man's spirit into man's soul and consequently it flows through his body and into the world. This is a continual process and creates a complete spiritual man. While the meaning of zoe life may seem obvious we should state that it refers to the God kind of life. It is an expression of the best and most complete type of life.

> 1 Corinthians 2:14 (NKJV) ¹⁴ *But the **natural man** does not receive the things of the Spirit of God, for they are foolishness to him; nor can he know them, because they are spiritually discerned.*

This term "**natural man**" is referring to soulish realm meaning the soul of man. This scripture is telling us that the natural man or our soul can't receive things from the spirit world directly. Only man's spirit can receive and interpret things from the spirit world.

So, the soul or "natural man" is the part of man's nonmaterial nature that makes him aware of his body and his natural, physical environment. The soul or "natural man" is also the medium that receives communication from his spirit and makes him aware of the spiritual environment.

We will see later how this flow of life in man has changed throughout history and the impact those changes have had on man and the rest of the world.

In summary, these are three different Greek references to life; zoe, psuche, and bios. We are using them to define life as we speak to the three parts of man: spirit, soul, and body. They all describe man's life but convey very different meanings.

Characteristics of Man's Spirit, Soul, and Body

So, we defined **life** source in each part of man but let's consider some other features and functions.

As we dissect the various components of man, we must remember that mankind was designed as a complete being in a manner that would allow life to flow from the throne of God into man's spirit, through his soul and body and the world.

We discussed the soul has a very close relationship with the body – after all the soul is the life source of the body.

Soul and spirit are distinctly different from each other but also very closely related, partly because both are invisible and nonmaterial and neither one can be seen with the eyes of our body. In that respect, they are opposite of the body which is material or physical.

Our spirit, soul, and body have specific purposes and functions and we will go into much greater detail. When God created Adam, He created him with purpose and all three parts of man to be in unity.

- **Adam's Body** – was in unison with the earth in which it came from, and his body communicates in the world with his five senses. His body was submitted to his soul, because his soul was his body's life source.

- **Adam's soul** – was in unison with his body and his soul directed his body. It was also in unison with his spirit, but it was his spirit that provided guidance and direction to his soul, because his spirit was its life source. Adam would process all of the goodness from God in his mind and intellectual processes, as well as in the richness of his emotions to align his will with God's will.

- **Adam's spirit** – was in unison with God and under God's authority as Adam received guidance and direction, righteousness, peace, and joy from God, because God was his life source. Consequently, Adam's spirit was on the throne of his being, meaning his spirit was in charge. As such his spirit provided guidance and authority over his soul. [Diagram 2]

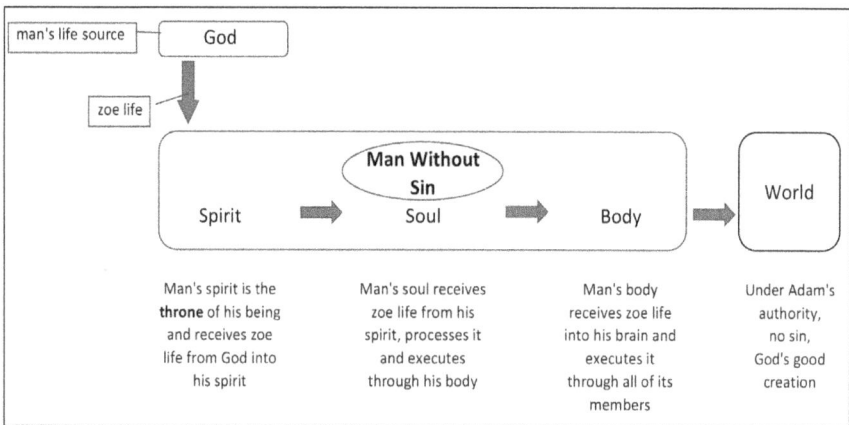

The diagram above displays the relationship of God and Adam, and the flow of life through Adam's being. It shows the structure of Adam's being and the process that God intended for Adam to establish his authority within his being and over the earth.

Adam's spirit had communion with God and received zoe life from God.

Adam's soul processed that zoe life through his intellect, will and emotions which are primary functions of the soul.

Adam's body expressed that zoe life as he interacted with Eve and all the rest of creation.

Information could flow up or down this process but had to flow through the established process. In other words, the spirit can't communicate directly to the body, it must go through the soul, and vice, versa. Also, the soul can't go directly to God, it must go through the man's spirit.

In other words, man's body communicates with the physical world, man's spirit communicates with the spirit world, and man's soul processes information from and through the body or spirit. You could also view the soul as the communications department or the medium or the joint connecting the spirit and body. An important note to remember; at this time in history there is no sin in Adam or in the world. Therefore, even worldly things can be communicated up/down the communication network all the way up to God.

So, in summary, we can see that God created Adam as a three-part being – spirit, soul, and body. But the emphasis is that Adam is a living soul. His spirit is God-conscious, his soul is self-conscious, and his body is world-conscious.

Now after God made Adam, He saw that Adam needed a mate, so he created a wife for him.

> *Genesis 2:18 (NKJV)* [18] *And the LORD God said, "It is not good that man should be alone; I will make him a helper comparable to him."*

Genesis 2:21-23 (NKJV) And the LORD God caused a
deep sleep to fall on Adam, and he slept; and He took one
of his ribs, and closed up the flesh in its place. ²² Then the
rib which the LORD God had taken from man He made
into a woman, and He brought her to the man.
²³ And Adam said:
"This is now bone of my bones
And flesh of my flesh;
She shall be called Woman,
Because she was taken out of Man."

This is the first couple, and they will be responsible for multiplying human beings on earth. Adam loved his wife and was thankful to God for her.

Difference Between Adam and Other Creatures

So now we know how Adam was made but what is the difference between Adam and all other creatures on earth or the angels for that matter?

> *Mankind is different than any other creature that*
> *God created.*

There are two categories of creatures, **heavenly** (celestial) and **earthly** (terrestrial).

Let's start with heavenly creatures which are angels and demons. All angels were created as spirit beings. In other words, no angel or demon has flesh and blood. We will discuss differences between fallen angels or demons later. They are all created beings, as they are not born from a mother because they do not mate and reproduce. They are spirit beings, and they have a soul. They can manifest temporarily in the appearance of a man, but they are still spirits because they do not have a body of flesh and blood.

All earthly creatures have one thing in common – they all have a body with flesh and blood. Even a young child can easily distinguish physical characteristics of animals just by seeing their bodies and they can identify a cat versus a dog, even though they are different sizes and colors. So, the body of earthly creatures can have distinctly different or unique features in appearance and functions, or they may have many similarities, but all earthly creatures have flesh and blood.

Additionally, God created earthly creatures with a soul. Their souls are also invisible but unlike mankind there is no scripture that states that any earthly creature's soul is eternal, except for mankind. I do not know of any scripture that states an animal can't be eternal. However, we do know that an animal's body dies and returns to dust, therefore we can conclude that sin has infiltrated animals as well. Therefore, it is likely their soul will also cease to exist. The souls of earthly creatures (just like their body) can be very different from one creature to another both in form and function. For example, a dog may have much more intelligence than a cow, or a monkey may express many more emotions than an alligator. But in all of them it is the soul that instructs the body what to do in all earthly creatures and their soul makes them self-conscious or aware of themselves.

> *Genesis 7:15 (NKJV) And they went into the ark to Noah, two by two, **of all flesh in which is the breath of life.***

As we discussed the breath of life can be referring to the soul.

> *Genesis 1:30 (CJB 2016)* [30] *And to every wild animal, bird in the air and creature crawling on the earth, in which there is **a living soul**, I am giving as food every kind of green plant." And that is how it was.*

The Complete Jewish Bible translation as shown above is referring to earthly creatures other than mankind in which there is a living soul.

Remember there are at least two primary functions of a soul.

1. To tell the body how and when to function to support physical life. For example, how to breathe, eat, digest food, and so on. The body itself does not provide that function, neither in mankind nor other creatures.

2. To be aware of itself or be self-conscious.

Beyond these two basic functions the soul of some creatures can be significantly different and more complex. This is certainly true for the soul of mankind.

Mankind is the only earthly creature that is a triune being. Specifically, we have a spirit, soul, and body. Mankind is also the only creature that was made in the image and likeness of God. That makes every person special to God!

The Nature of Mankind

What does it mean when we talk about nature? Our modern society has developed many opinions and uses regarding this simple word. When used generically or in a broad view of the world many people use this word as their god (the god of nature or mother nature). Some individuals want to become one with the nature of the universe. This can be a dangerous viewpoint if we don't capture or understand it correctly. Let us start by bringing some clarity. God, (Elohim), created the universe: the stars, sun, and moon. He created the earth and the sea and all the living plants and creatures in it. His creation is just that – His creation, not another god. In other words, God or Elohim is my God. The world or nature that He created is not my god, it is His creation for us to enjoy with Him.

For this discussion to define mankind, we will use the definition for nature as the inherent character or constitution of a person, creature, or thing or simply the type or main characteristics of something.

We can use this definition for all living things including characteristics of God or anything that God has created.

> *Genesis 1:25 (NKJV)* [25] *And God made the beast of the earth according to its kind, cattle according to its kind, and everything that creeps on the earth according to its kind. And God saw that it was good.*

As we look at this verse "according to its kind" refers to its nature. For example, a dog is a dog, and it has the nature of a dog. When dogs mate they give birth to dogs not cats. As such a dog does not have the desire to mate with a cat because it is not in its nature. It is a dog's nature to bark. You cannot train a cat to bark because it's not in their nature. In other words, God created each creature with its own nature or individual characteristics. Each species has its own nature, and each individual dog or cat also has its own unique characteristics. The nature of a dog is displayed in its physical characteristics including its gene pool or DNA. As such the DNA of a dog also includes the way it thinks. For example, look at their natural defense system - a cat has claws and scratches, and a dog will bite, it doesn't try to scratch you with its paw. These are natural instincts embedded into their nature.

We can further define human nature as the fundamental dispositions and characteristics—including ways of thinking, feeling, and acting, that humans are said to have naturally. For example, when a baby is born it doesn't know how to walk or talk but our DNA is such that we inherently know and develop to walk on our feet and use our voice to communicate. And even though God didn't provide written instructions to parents on how to train babies to walk and talk, we are able to figure it out naturally because that is our nature.

We all easily recognize walking and talking are two basic elements of our nature, but it helps us to understand that our natural instincts or human nature incorporates all parts of our being.

In our body scientists can see many aspects of our nature in a genetic code referred to as our DNA. Scientists have been discovering many traits within all manners of physical life including man, animals and even plants through DNA. So, you could say DNA is a quantifiable method of identifying the nature of something with a natural body. However, these scientists can only see DNA in our physical body because our soul and spirit are invisible, so scientists have no means to measure the nature of these parts of our being.

But we see below the Word of God tells us something about our invisible nature.

> *Romans 2:14-15 (NKJV)* [14] *for when Gentiles, who do not have the law, by **nature** do the things in the law, these, although not having the law, are a law to themselves,* [15] *who show the work of the law written in their hearts, their conscience also bearing witness, and between themselves their thoughts accusing or else excusing them)*

The apostle Paul is giving us an example here by confirming that God has written His law in man's heart which is simply describing part of the nature of man. This is another way of saying God made us in His image and likeness, or we could also say according to His nature.

So, our nature can be defined by specific details. For example, it is the nature of mankind to walk upright on two feet. In a similar way, it is the nature of a dog to walk on four feet. These are natural means for us to travel because we are born that way. As a baby, we still need to develop our ability to walk but it is natural to us, and every person learns to walk.

But our nature can also be defined from a higher viewpoint or perspective. For example, when God created Adam, He created him to be sinless. He also created Adam to receive God's goodness and fellowship with

God through his spirit. And God created Adam's spirit to be the head of his being. In other words, Adam's spirit was dependent on God and his spirit was the leader of his being. That was Adam's nature.

Unfortunately, we will soon see that Adam changed his nature.

CHAPTER 3

The Garden of Eden

Adam and Eve lived in a perfectly peaceful, joy filled, and loving environment. There was no awareness of sin, no death, no guilt, no marital arguments, no financial problems, just a life filled with righteousness, peace, joy, and friendship with each other and most importantly friendship with God. Even the animals like lions and bears were friendly with them. God walked and talked with them in the afternoons and together God and man both enjoyed His creation. They had no lack for anything, nor did they have any form of anxiety in any part of their lives. Adam and Eve were living in the perfect life that God designed for them. His plan and desires were for them to live like this forever. We recognize that this time period of God's creation is known as the "time of innocence." Meaning that there was no knowledge or awareness of evil, sin, guilt, or shame. Everything in their life was bliss, happiness, joyful and perfect just as God created it. Since there was no presence of sin on the earth Adam and Eve enjoyed a loving relationship with God.

God Planted a Garden

God planted a special garden for Adam and Eve to live in. In the Garden of Eden, Adam lived in perfect harmony with himself, his wife, his environment and with God. His total being was in unison with the universe.

Adam and Eve walked and talked with God. Adam and Eve enjoyed a wonderful relationship with God in their original created status.

> *Genesis 2:8-9 (NKJV) The LORD God planted a garden eastward in Eden, and there He put the man whom He had formed. ⁹ And out of the ground the LORD God made **every tree grow** that is pleasant to the sight and good for food. The tree of life was also in the midst of the garden, and the tree of the knowledge of good and evil.*

God truly provided abundantly for Adam and Eve. He planted this garden that provided fruit from all the different trees that were good for food. All the trees in the garden of Eden were fruit bearing trees. Most likely this would have included apple trees, orange trees, and avocado trees just to name a few. Can you imagine the quality of fruit from God's Garden that He personally planted? God made every tree grow that is pleasant to the sight and good for food. Everyone is aware that scientists have identified specific nutrients in fruits that can provide nourishment for our bodies. For example, orange trees produce oranges and oranges produce vitamin C. We also know that Vitamin C supports and strengthens our immune system. The fruit from this garden helped them to maintain a healthy supply of nutrition of all types to sustain a healthy life.

However, in verse 9, God calls out two very specific trees and God is identifying them as being different from all the other fruit trees. It appears both trees provide a different type of nourishment.

> *Genesis 2:16-17 (NKJV) And the LORD God commanded the man, saying, "Of **every tree** of the garden you may freely eat; ¹⁷ but of the tree of the knowledge of good and evil you shall not eat, for in the day that you eat of it you shall surely die."*

God's command in verse 16 is vividly clear – He says "of **every** tree of the garden you may freely eat". This clearly includes the tree of life. He also follows up immediately in verse 17 *"but of the tree of the knowledge of good and evil you shall not eat, for in the day that you eat of it you shall surely die."*

As God is giving Adam instructions about these two trees, He is encouraging Adam and telling him to do the right thing and freely eat of all the trees of the garden including the tree of life. In verse 17, on the other hand, He is giving Adam a clear and firm warning to not eat of the tree of knowledge of good and evil for in the day you eat of it you will surely die. While God's command and His desire is clear He is also allowing Adam the freedom to choose death. The principle behind these two trees is a core topic throughout the Bible. These trees essentially represent **life and death**, and they also represent **dependence and independence**. The fruit of these two specific trees are seeds of spiritual truths that can be seen throughout the Bible. Throughout the history of mankind every person ever born is symbolically responsible to choose which tree they desire to eat from, and the decision we make will determine where our eternal home will be. Let's take a closer look at each of these trees individually.

Tree of Life

To look at life or the tree of life we first need to start by recognizing that God is the source of life. God is life, and He created life, and He is eternal. When God created Adam, He created him without sin in his spirit, soul, and body. God gave abundance of life to Adam, and God's life was able to freely flow through Adam's being, that is because Adam did not know sin. As such Adam was able to enjoy a wonderful relationship with God. They walked and talked together. If Adam could have refrained from eating from either of these two trees he would have lived with God for eternity because he didn't know sin, therefore he would have never died. It is Adam's sin that gave death its legal authority on earth. If Adam would have refrained from God's one restriction and not sinned, then death would never have had access to the earth or any beings in the world. But Adam would have always been vulnerable to eating the fruit from the tree of knowledge of good and evil. However, if he would have eaten from the tree of life first, he would have secured his life in eternity with God.

Make note that even though Adam enjoyed a wonderful relationship with God, the Holy Spirit did not dwell in Adam's spirit. This means that Adam did not possess the Nature of God, but because Adam did not know sin, he could maintain a relationship with God and the life of God could flow through him. We, as born-again believers do possess the very Nature of God because the Holy Spirit dwells inside of us. This is what Adam could have received if he ate from the tree of life.

What is the tree of life? We saw in Genesis 2:9 that it is a fruit tree, and now in 3:22 we see that the fruit it produces will provide immortality when it is eaten.

> *Genesis 3:22 (NKJV)* ²² *Then the LORD God said, "Behold, the man has become like one of Us, to know good and evil. And now, lest he put out his hand and take also of **the tree of life, and eat, and live forever**"—*

God made this choice for Adam clear, right in the beginning. If Adam would have chosen the tree of life first, he could have secured eternal life with God. But now God had to remove the tree of life from the garden because God did not want Adam to have eternal life without Him. In other words, the fruit of the tree of life would have sealed mankind's fate in eternity in the state that he was in at the time he consumed the fruit, whether it be with God or without God.

What else do we know from scriptures about the tree of life?

> *Proverbs 11:30 (NKJV)* ³⁰ *The fruit of the righteous is a **tree of life**, And he who wins souls is wise.*

To understand this scripture, it is important to recognize that *"the fruit of the righteous"* is referring to Godly righteousness not the righteousness of man. The true fruit of Godly righteousness produces life.

> *Revelation 2:7 (NKJV)* [7] *"He who has an ear, let him hear what the Spirit says to the churches. To him who overcomes I will give to eat from the **tree of life**, which is in the midst of the Paradise of God."*

> *Revelation 22:2 (NKJV)* [2] *In the middle of its street, and on either side of the river, was the **tree of life**, which bore twelve fruits, each tree yielding its fruit every month. The leaves of the tree were for the healing of the nations.*

These are a few direct scriptures about the tree of life. The fruit of this tree was only available to Adam and Eve before they sinned and now, we see it is available to all the saints at the end of the millennium when our salvation is complete. It is a source of Divine nutrition that ensures immortality and healing. It is a source of life coming from God Himself. God clearly stated His desire is that we draw life from Him as our source of life.

The point I am establishing here is how significant the difference is between these two trees and the fruit they produce. While it may seem obvious to choose life (and it is) many people are like Adam and Eve and chose death. And another issue to consider is that a person cannot stroll through life assuming that they have chosen life through default. This is a very intentional decision that every person is required to consciously make.

Tree of Knowledge of Good and Evil

Note verse 9 says "**every tree**" is pleasant to their sight and good for food. The tree of knowledge of good and evil did not look any better than the rest of the trees. They all looked good and desirable. Adam and Eve were not restricted to second best, they had full access to God's best.

In other words, the tree of knowledge of good and evil was not more or less appealing, all the trees were appealing to Adam and Eve. God gave one command – *".... you must not eat from the tree of knowledge of good and evil, for when you eat from it you will surely die."* God's command and the consequences of disobedience were vividly clear. There was not any confusion regarding this manner.

It is important to recognize that this command from God to not eat the fruit of the tree of knowledge of good or evil was not to test or evaluate their obedience or to tempt Adam and Eve. It was an opportunity for them to have a choice. True love requires that we choose to accept His love and love Him in return.

Let's take a closer look at what the tree of knowledge of good and evil represents. The tree of death is very subtle. Although this tree brings forth death it is not called the tree of death. We can see there are three things related to the name of this tree – knowledge, good, and evil. As I have continued to study this, I am sure most people would agree that we like knowledge and good, but we don't like evil. We consider good and evil to be two distinct categories. While good and evil have different meanings, the Bible is telling us here, they are in the same category and are part of the same tree whose fruit produces death. Nonetheless, this indicates that our first primary focus should be towards recognizing the distinction between **life** and **death** first; before we begin considering **good** and **evil**.

We see that knowledge and good are coupled with evil. We could say that these three words are in the same family or even say they are three sisters who work together to bring forth **death**, which of course is the opposite of **life**. We will look deeper into this topic in other chapters, but I want to expose a larger perspective here that we can build upon later.

Early in Genesis we are introduced to the importance of life and death, and we see the seed of life and the seed of death through these two trees.

Then at the end of the book of Revelation we see the consummation of life and death. Death, referred to as the last enemy, is cast into the lake of fire (hell) for eternity. Then we see that life abounds in the New Jerusalem for eternity. In it there is a river of life with the tree of life growing in it for eternity. [Diagram 3]

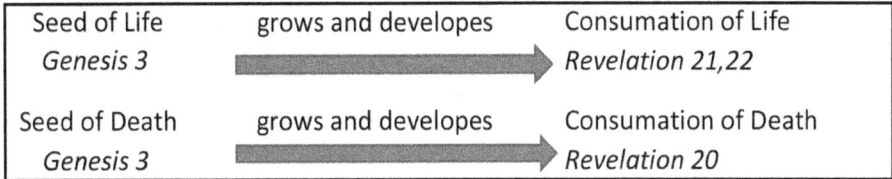

Seed of Life	grows and developes	Consumation of Life
Genesis 3		Revelation 21,22
Seed of Death	grows and developes	Consumation of Death
Genesis 3		Revelation 20

The seed of life is sown in the beginning of the Bible. It is revealed in the tree of life and in the Seed of Eve which is referencing Jesus Christ. The Seed grows and develops throughout the Bible, and in the end of the Bible it consummates in the harvest of life. Likewise, the seed of death is also sown at the beginning of the Bible. It is revealed in the tree of knowledge of good and evil and in the seed from Satan which is sin. It also continues to grow throughout the earth and at the end of the Bible it consumes its harvest and is thrown into the lake of fire for eternity. As such we can trace the line of life and the line of death throughout the Bible. [Diagram 4]

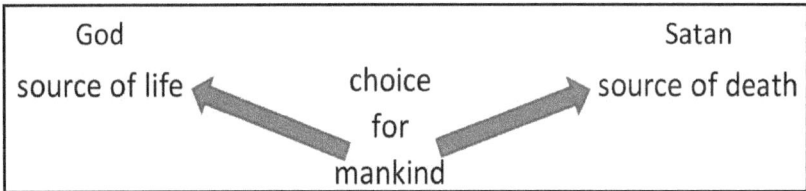

God		Satan
source of life	choice	source of death
	for	
	mankind	

We see in Genesis chapter 2 a triangular situation where man faces two sources: God as the source of life, and Satan as the source of death. We see a continuation of this triangular situation in Romans chapters 5-8. This will become more clear and easier to understand as we introduce more information in the coming chapters. The conclusion of this point is that our first focus should be recognizing which tree to eat from - the choice of **life** or **death** and the importance of choosing life.

Here is another important view of the difference between these two trees and their fruit. The tree of life implies *dependence* on God. On the other hand, the fruit of the tree of knowledge of good and evil implies *independence* from God. Adam essentially established his desire to strengthen his own mind, will, and emotions to gain his own independence from God.

The tree of life first portrays God as the source of life to man. As we analyze all matters related to life, we see that many matters of life require **dependence**. A person doesn't graduate from all matters of life. For example, eating is a matter of life. After you have eaten a very large meal that was filled with nutrition and energy sources, you can't say, I don't need to eat ever again because I'm filled up. Simply put, your body will use up or burn off the nutrition and energy you ate, and you will need to replenish it to sustain your physical life. The sustaining of your physical life is dependent on eating another meal. Breathing is another matter of life that is dependent on regular flow of oxygen to sustain life. The matters of eating, drinking, and breathing of course are all dependent matters that we do not graduate from. We will always be dependent on those matters to sustain life in our current physical bodies. So, if we choose to accept life, it includes our spirit and soul, and our life will continue into eternity which is well beyond our physical body. That brings us all back to the need to put our trust and dependance on God.

> *John 15:5 (NKJV)* [5] *"I am the vine, you are the branches. He who abides in Me, and I in him, bears much fruit; for without Me you can do nothing.*

Clearly, we see here that to sustain life we must stay connected to the Vine which is Jesus. It is important to stress again and again that the tree of life signifies God as the source of life to man. Once man accepts God as his life source, he becomes dependent on God to sustain his life. This is the place in life that we find safety, security, peace, joy, and righteousness. Simply put it is putting our trust in Him.

Now, one of the effects of eating the fruit from the tree of knowledge of good and evil is that it would over nourish parts of their soul and provide them with an unrealistic expectation of their own abilities. Adam and Eve wanted their **independence** from God because they thought they could be just like God by themselves, and therefore they did not think they needed Him. And just as God warned them, that decision would result in their death. That death is essentially separation from God, who is their source of life.

In summary of these two trees, the fruit of the tree of life was their life source and would have nourished their spirit as the Holy Spirit (God's life) would have been the eternal nourishment from the fruit they would have received. On the other hand, the fruit of the tree of knowledge of good and evil would become their source of life and provide over nourishment to their soul and bring immediate death to their spirit.

The Temptation and Sin

Now remember this time of Adam and Eve's life was a time of innocence. They had no awareness of evil or sin. Remember each day when God was creating, He reviewed His creation at the end of each day and said, "*it is good*" and at the end of the sixth day after creating Adam and Eve He said, "*it is very good.*"

God was aware of the effect that the fruit of knowledge of good and evil would have on them. That is why He commanded them to stay away from it. But He had to allow Adam and Eve to have a "free will." True love requires that we choose to love, which provides for a good relationship because both parties truly desire the relationship. Therefore, He provided this opportunity for them in order that they could show their love for Him. If we are forced to serve someone or something, it is not a product of love. God did not create us as robots that He programmed to be obedient or disobedient. God created us as individual human beings with our own unique personality and with everything needed to make our own individual decision to love God. He could have created us as a robot, but He chose to give us the freedom to choose. He also made it clear what the consequences of our choices were. The choice of **life** or **death** is still required for every person today. Through faith, acceptance, and trust in Jesus as our Lord we can live with Him for eternity – this is of course *dependence* on Jesus Christ. If we do not choose Him, we will live for eternity without Him. If we don't purposely choose Jesus, the default is automatically choosing *independence* from God, when we choose to do it our way instead of following the Way, which is Jesus Christ. If we stop and consider it, eternity is a long time, it's forever.

Adam and Eve both understood God's command to not eat the forbidden fruit. So, they obeyed Him and enjoyed the wonderful life God provided, until this one day when the serpent tempted Eve. If we look at this scene from a historical, big picture perspective it can be difficult to understand why they sinned, but if we zoom in more and humble ourselves, all of us can relate to times that we have made similar decisions. Their life was so good. They had no need to eat from the tree of knowledge of good and evil. They had all the knowledge they needed. All of Adam and Eves spiritual needs, emotional needs, and physical needs were supplied by God with fullness. The problem began when Eve opened a door in temptation, and she was deceived.

> *Genesis 3:1-5 (NKJV) Now the serpent was more cunning than any beast of the field which the LORD God had made. And he said to the woman, "Has God indeed*

*said, 'You shall not eat of **every tree** of the garden'?"*
² And the woman said to the serpent, "We may eat the fruit of the trees of the garden; ³ but of the fruit of the tree which is in the midst of the garden, God has said, 'You shall not eat it, nor shall you touch it, lest you die.' "
⁴ Then the serpent said to the woman, "You will not surely die. ⁵ For God knows that in the day you eat of it your eyes will be opened, and you will be like God, knowing good and evil."

Adam and Eve understood God's only restriction – In fact in verse three, we see that Eve tries to repeat God's command to the serpent, and she quoted it back to the serpent. However, she made at least four key errors.

1. The first and biggest error is that while she identified the tree of knowledge of good and evil, she never even acknowledged the tree of life. Both trees were identified as unique trees in the garden. If she had eaten from it first, we wouldn't be having this discussion.

2. Eve reduced God's "freely eat" to "may eat."

3. She downplayed God's emphasis on the availability of fruit from every tree but one.

4. She added "not touching" to God's prohibition against "not eating."

The serpent did not command her to eat the fruit, nor did he force her to eat it because he did not have authority to command her. Satan also understood this element of God's creation and that mankind had to choose life or death. Therefore, he simply questioned her; did God really say you must not eat from **every tree** in the garden? He changed God's command just a little by adding **every tree** instead of **the tree**. Then the serpent directly lied to her as if he were the authority - ... *"you will surely* *not die."* Then he raised the question of God's motives – *"For God knows that in the day you eat of it your eyes will be opened, and you will be like God, knowing good and evil."* The devil will often tell **partial truths** just as in this case. The serpent or Satan approached Eve as if he wanted to be her friend and help her. The serpent planted a seed of doubt and even though at first, she partially responded appropriately by trying to restate what she thought God really said…., but she slightly missed it and opened the door that allowed a seed of doubt to stay and grow and created a thought. Then she was deceived when the serpent said, "surely you will not die."

As she dwelt on this thought the fruit became more appetizing to her and as she continued to contemplate the situation, the seed of doubt continued to grow.

> *Genesis 3:6 (NKJV) So when the woman saw that the tree was good for food, that it was pleasant to the eyes, and a tree desirable to make one wise, she took of its fruit and ate. She also gave it to her husband with her, and he ate.*

Now in verse six, Eve sees that the fruit looks good for food, and it is appealing to her appetite (her body). This scripture says that she saw the tree was good for food and pleasant to the eyes. The word pleasant in Hebrew can be translated to describe food that is desired, bounty, craving, greed. It indicates the longings of a person's heart, its cravings. This is describing that it is appealing to her emotions and mind (her soul). And then it says a tree desirable to make one wise." The serpent told her she would be wise – just like God – pride of life. Is this a spiritual attack creating desire to be like a god?

> *1 John 2:16 (NKJV) [16] For all that is in the world—the lust of the flesh, the lust of the eyes, and the pride of life—is not of the Father but is of the world.*

In this scripture the Apostle John is telling us these three things that are in this world, and that they are not of the Father. It was Satan that brought sin into the world. Sin was not part of God's creation on earth. This was a time of innocence. Adam and Eve were given authority to kick Satan out, but they allowed him to bring sin into the earth. They were not viewing Satan as an adversary because he approached them as a friend. They weren't seeing Satan for who he was, a liar, thief, and murderer.

The lust of the flesh – Eve saw that it was good for food, appealing to her appetite.

Lust of the eyes – as she looked at it through her eyes (commonly referred to as window to the soul) it looked pleasant to her eyes as she reasoned it in her mind, and her emotions felt good, and through her will, she was determined to eat it.

Pride of life – Eve saw it was desirable to make one wise. This word pride can be described as self-confidence, an empty assurance, which trusts in its own power and resources and shamefully despises and violates divine laws. This word "life" in the Greek is bios. It infers life of the flesh which can incorporate the body and soul.

This scripture in 1 John 2:16 seems to explain how the devil tempted Eve. And they all have a root in the fleshly desires.

The spirit man was affected because of the sin of the fleshly soul and body. Satan pursued Eve's body and soul. It was an indirect attack to her spirit. Deceiving her and enticing her to eat fruit of the tree of knowledge of good and evil was the only access that Satan had to approach her because he did not have authority to require her to eat it. It is also important to note that she could have stopped this temptation at any moment. She had full authority over this situation.

Notice that the serpent did not appear to Eve as a lying, deceitful, ugly spirit that was proposing or threatening to steal from her, kill her, and destroy her. He was not carrying a pitchfork. The Bible says he was more cunning than any other beast in the field. He deceived her by acting friendly as if he were trying to help her and he got her to look at herself instead of God, and he tricked her. How many times has he tricked us and deceived us? There is much to learn about basic spiritual warfare if we stop and be aware of the devils' tricks. Let us keep our focus and dependence on God and stay true to Him and be aware of the devils' tricks and avoid him.

She then gave the fruit to Adam, and he ate the fruit. Now, we know Eve was deceived by Satan. It appears that Adam watched this story of Eve's deception unfold and he did not say anything. In fact, Adam had full authority given to him from God and Adam could have stopped this situation at any time as well. There is no sign showing that he too was deceived.

> *1 Timothy 2:14 (NKJV)* [14] *And Adam was not deceived, but the woman being deceived, fell into transgression.*

This scripture tells us that Adam was not deceived. After a deeper look into this scripture the word deceived is used twice. Each usage carries a slightly different perspective meaning that they are measured in different degrees. Perhaps the meaning is that Eve was more significantly deceived and didn't grasp the depth of her decision to eat the fruit. Adam on the other hand, had a clearer understanding of the sin he was committing and the consequences thereof. In other words, Adam was tempted and fell into that temptation but he understood more of the decision he was making and that it was a direct violation against God.

Adam could have and should have stopped Eve from eating the fruit. We do not know for sure what all his thoughts were during this whole event, but Adam made his own clear decision to eat the forbidden fruit. He was fully aware of the consequences and could have stopped Satan and kicked him out of the garden altogether. Even after Eve ate the fruit, Adam had the authority to stop Satan and put an end to this situation. This was one of the responsibilities Adam had as ruler of the earth – to keep predators away. Satan didn't belong in the earth and Adam should have just kicked him out.

To be clear, the choice Adam made was life or death, or in other words God or Satan. To repeat again, this was not a test of Adam's obedience to God, it was a choice to accept or reject God. Satan tempted Adam to the point that Adam switched his allegiance to Satan rather than to God. We know that Adam wasn't deceived but he was tempted. Adam started looking at himself and wanted to be like God and wanted to have this knowledge of good and evil. He thought that if he chose to have knowledge of good and evil, he wouldn't need to rely on God to provide zoe life into his spirit because he would possess this knowledge in his own soul. He therefore turned his allegiance to Satan instead of God.

Adam's Awareness

Again, we don't know all of Adam's thoughts. Based on scripture it is appropriate to assume that he understood and realized he was making a choice of life or death. Keep in mind the concept of death was not well known at that time in history. Adam and Eve had not seen or experienced any type of death. It would appear that Adam's knowledge of death was that it would be a separation from God. Perhaps he didn't realize that it was for eternity. Most likely he didn't think that far down the road. Or perhaps he just thought it will be ok as soon as he obtains all this knowledge of good and evil. After all he was already pretty smart and felt like he would be able to manage things ok. And he had a great friend in Eve. So, she could fill God's role as a friend. Maybe

Adam was a bit upset because he thought that God was holding out on him as Satan suggested.

How many millions or billions of people around the world throughout history have considered similar thoughts? Or variations of these thoughts like; I have never accepted Jesus and my life is just fine, or I'm a good person and have lots of friends just like me that don't believe in Jesus, so maybe we will just party in hell for eternity … .hahaha.

When people's eyes are opened, they can see the severity of the consequences. It is much easier to choose life before it's not too late.

Satan and God Are Not Equal

Before moving forward let us consider a basic foundational truth. While we are discussing a choice between Satan and God, we are not comparing them as equals. Far from it – we are comparing a part of their nature. Life is God's nature. Death is Satan's nature. We see this principle throughout the Bible. In this view it is important to note that this element of God's nature and Satan's nature are opposites but note that it is the nature that we are comparing, not the persons. Satan is not the opposite of God. God stands alone as the Almighty. He is the creator of life, He is, always was, and will be forever. Satan is a spirit being that was created by God. Lucifer, which is Satan's original name, rebelled against God and as a result lost his relationship with the Almighty God and Lucifer essentially died because he lost his relationship with God. Satan did not have authority on the earth. As we already reviewed, God gave Adam the responsibility to rule this world. That said there were changes after Adam sinned and we will discuss those changes later.

CHAPTER 4

The Effect of Adam's Sin

Try to imagine life without knowledge of sin. This is not easy for most humans today because we were born with sin and it's in the world and all around us. Even still, imagine the peace, love, joy, righteousness, wisdom, and every good thing Adam and Eve received from God flowed unhindered through their spirit into their soul and body in perfect harmony. God's communication and relationship with Adam and Eve was wonderful in every way because they did not have knowledge of good and evil. Also, their relationship with each other as husband and wife was wonderful. There was perfect peace in the world and every part of their lives.

However, Adam and Eve rebelled against God. God had created humanity in His likeness and image; but being in His likeness and image was not enough for Adam and Eve: they wanted to be just like God — but they wanted to be independent from God, to do with their lives as they pleased. Their rebellion overturned the order of creation.

> *The choice that Adam made was to seek himself or his own soul as his life source rather than choosing God as his source of life.*

For that reason, God judged Adam and Eve. God expelled them from the garden. Thus, humanity began a journey away from the presence of

God. The order of creation was broken. Relationships were also broken. Things are not the way they were supposed to be.

God said if they ate from the tree of knowledge of good and evil, on that day they would surely die. But what does that really mean?

When Adam ate the forbidden fruit what part of him died? His body did not die right away. In fact, he physically lived 930 years. His soul did not die because his **mind** remained aware of his surroundings. Adam's memory was intact because he remembered all the names of the animals. His **emotions** did not die because many emotions were continually displayed through him and his family. His **willpower** did not die because they continued to do as they pleased. So, what was it that died immediately when he sinned?

As we look at the effects on Adam from eating the fruit of the tree of knowledge of good and evil, we will see that Adam's spirit, soul, and body were all affected. Let us look at how all three dimensions of Adam's being (spirit, soul, body) were impacted. And then we can look at the effects upon the rest of the world.

Adam's Spirit Died

We should first answer the question - What is death? It is the disconnection from the source of life. When Adam and Eve ate the forbidden fruit, they immediately experienced spiritual death. According to God's design, Adam and Eve's relationship with God was through their spirit. God is Spirit and His relationship with man was through man's spirit. As we have discussed Adam's spirit ruled his being. Through his spirit he was alive to God and received an abundance of life or zoe life which is all the good things from God through his spirit. But when Adam rebelled against God his spirit died. Adam's spirit did not cease to exist – he still had a spirit because Adam's spirit was and is eternal, but it was dead to

God. The death of Adam's spirit had a continual and profound impact on the nature of mankind.

As we have seen, before their sin, Adam and Eve's spirit flowed perfectly with God. God is spirit and He generally communicates with man through man's spirit. It was Adam's spirit that communicated directly with God. God did not talk directly to Adam's soul or his body but to his spirit. When God created Adam and Eve, they had no knowledge of sin.

So, we can affirm, the answer to our earlier question, is that it was Adam's spirit that died that day. His death was because of his rebellion against God, which caused Adam's spirit to be disconnected from his true-life source which is God or in other words he had a lack of divine nourishment. Adam's sin was not a simple matter of disobedience because he ate fruit that he was not supposed to eat. Adam had a choice of receiving an abundance of life from God **or** death due to rebellion towards God by seeking **independence from God**. Adam understood that this was a direct rebellion against God and the significance of his decision was death via terminating his direct relationship with God.

It appears Adam understood that God created him to rule the world if he kept his trust in God. It appears Satan convinced Adam that if he transferred his allegiance to Satan by eating this forbidden fruit, then Adam would have the one thing he was lacking – knowledge of good and evil. As Satan told Adam, he could be just like God if he ate this fruit, and therefore Adam didn't think he would need God.

When Adam sinned, his relationship with God changed. God was Adam's spiritual source of life. When Adam sinned and rebelled against God then the effect was that **Adam terminated** his spiritual relationship with God. As mentioned earlier the term, died, can be described as "cease to exist" and in this case, it was Adam and Eve's communion or relationship with God that ceased to exist. It was the flow of life coming directly from God into Adam's spirit that ceased. God cannot or will not co-exist with sin. Adam's relationship with God was now substantially different. Adam chose to obtain knowledge of good and evil from the tree that produces death, instead of receiving life from God. Adam still had a spirit, but his spirit was not in communion with God. As such it is common to say Adam's spirit was dead to God because now, he did not have the truth and life of God's Spirit flowing through him. All this was Adam's decision. As this sin of rebellion entered Adam's being, death followed. Adam's spirit linked him to the Spirit of God. That communication link from God to Adam was now broken, and the life that flowed from God into Adam's spirit had stopped flowing and his spirit died.

Adam's Soul is Changed

As we look at the changes in Adam's soul let's remember that the three primary faculties of the soul are our mind, emotions, and will. Our mind incorporates our intellectual realm or reasoning. Our emotions incorporate feelings, and our will is where we choose. In other words, our soul is where we think, feel, and choose.

Man's soul does not have a direct relationship with God. Remember, God is spirit, and God chose to have His relationship with man through man's spirit because that was the way He created mankind. When Adam sinned, and he rebelled against God, his spirit lost communion or his relationship with God, the effect was that Adam's spirit forfeited his Godly authority over his being. Man in his away-from-God state can also give the spirit left within him to evil such as sorcery, fortune telling, and other spiritual influences. From this point in history, frequently man's spirit is subjected to the dictates of his fleshly, soulish desires.

Because man's spirit is dead to God, it seems obvious that his spirit is no longer on the throne of his being, or in other words not in charge anymore.

Man With Sin			

God	spirit ⟷	soul ⟷	body ⟷	world
Our Creator, Giver of life, Spirit	Man's spirit is dead to God. But it is still present in his being	Man's soul - his mind, emotions, and will are on the throne of his being	Soul & body are united as flesh. Sin is part of the DNA of man's flesh	Under Satan's authority, sin is rampant, death is reigning

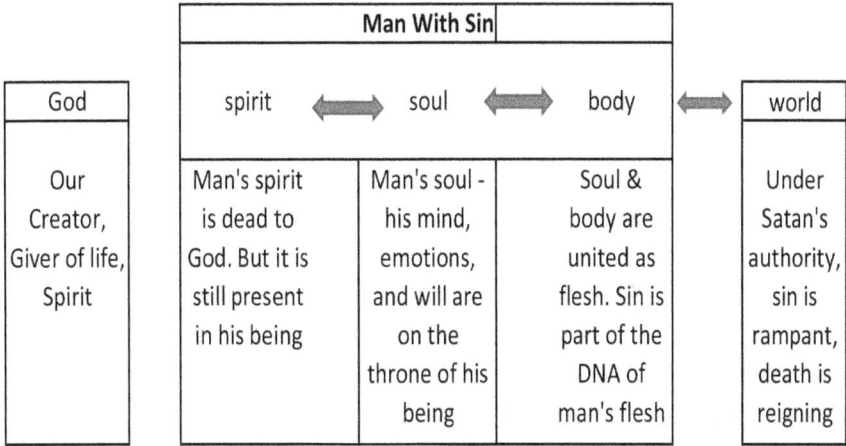

God created mankind with the ability to choose. Adam chose death. By choosing to eat the fruit from the tree of knowledge of good and evil he was choosing to change the structured process of the flow of life that God created.

Now that Adam's spirit died, and Adam possessed this knowledge of good and evil, his soul used this new knowledge and was determined to overthrow his spirit and be on the throne of his being. Adam traded the flow of life from God for the knowledge of good and evil. That said, frequently his fleshly desires also arise from members of his fleshly body as well, and they share the throne.

> *Genesis 3:7 (NKJV) ⁷ Then the eyes of both of them were opened, and they knew that they were naked; and they sewed fig leaves together and made themselves coverings.*

The first effect of their sin that we see here in verse seven is that their eyes were opened. This is not a reference to their physical eyes. They were both seeing with their physical eyes before and after their sin. This scripture is referring to their souls. The forbidden fruit they ate provided nutrition to their souls or perhaps we should say it poisoned their souls.

Either way it provoked changes in their souls and they now had the ability to see and have knowledge of good and evil.

God gave Adam authority to rule everything in the world. As such God provided all the knowledge and guidance that Adam needed to rule the world through his spirit, but Adam still had to process that knowledge and guidance in his soul. God created all three parts of man to work together in unity in the structured format and manner that we were designed to function. Adam's decision to eat this fruit, changed that structure and this change wasn't for the good of mankind. Most likely Adam had a significantly larger soul capacity before his sin. Being the ruler of the world is a big job and it can be easy to overlook the requirements of his job. We will expand on this later, but the point here is that it is likely that some parts of man's soul were awakened from Adam's sin and other parts were suppressed.

After Adam and Eve ate the forbidden fruit, they were ashamed and covered their nakedness with fig leaves. This was their attempt to hide their shame or in other words, make themselves righteous and acceptable before God by covering their unrighteousness. Then they heard God walking in the garden and so they hid from God because they were still ashamed, and they knew these fig leaves were not a sufficient covering. This was an initial sign of how Adam and Eve would begin showing their **independence** from God and how they made their own decisions. Still today when people sin, just like Adam and Eve, they hide from God because all of mankind inherently knows the righteousness of God and that He hates sin, so we try to hide sin, and many still focus on making ourselves righteous. But we are not capable of doing that ourselves. We can be self-righteous but that does not meet the standards of God's righteousness.

Adam and Eve's knowledge of good and evil made them aware of their nakedness and they were ashamed. It was their shame that caused them to hide from God. Their soul was awakened and supercharged because of eating the fruit of the tree of knowledge of good and evil. Before their sin, Adam, and Eve had no shame. Just like a baby or toddler they were naked and were comfortable in their innocence. Because of their sin, their innocence was removed.

This new knowledge of good and evil gave them what they were seeking – **independence from God**. Just like God they now had knowledge of good and evil, but this knowledge came with a significant price. It cost them their life! And now the first fruit they recognize from this knowledge is shame. In other words, when they changed their allegiance to Satan, they immediately obtained knowledge about themselves. This is a function of their soul which is self-consciousness.

Afterward, God in His love and mercy provided grace and made garments from animal skin to take the place of the fig leaves that Adam and Eve made. It appears that Adam may have repented, and God initiated the first blood sacrifice to atone for their sins. That would provide a covering for their sin but would not change the effects of sin in their being, or the effects it has in the world. We see a facet of God's character in this blood sacrifice as He offers His grace to Adam and Eve. Nonetheless, God still had to enforce justice because He is a just God.

Adam and Eve's spirit was dead to God and not ruling in a Godly manner or in other words, not providing the God life to their soul properly because they were not hearing and following the voice of God. Instead, they reasoned in their own minds (without God) what is good and evil instead of getting their information, knowledge, and guidance directly from God and being **dependent** on God as their source of everything that pertains to life. In other words, their souls were not able to process life issues properly because their spirits were not providing life guidance and their flesh was infected by their new sin nature.

Adam's sin had a tremendous impact on all of humanity in the physical, soulish, and spiritual realm. When Adam rebelled and ate the forbidden fruit, he chose death. God's original purpose was that the **human soul** should receive and assimilate in truth the substance of the spiritual life that He provided through Adam's spirit. God gave soulish gifts to men so that they might take in God's knowledge to flow through his intellect and emotions and align his own will with God's will. The key point is that Adam was originally designed to take in God's knowledge and guidance directly from God.

Through his spirit Adam **depended** on God to receive an abundant supply of truth and life directly from God. That truth and life then flowed into his soul and was processed in his soul. That meant Adam considered and processed these truths and life with his intellect, emotions, and his will. Since it was pure truth from God, it flowed perfectly from his soul into his body. Adam's soul was submitted to his spirit, and his body was submitted to his soul, or in other words, his body followed the directions from his soul. That means sickness and disease, or sin or death was not entering into his soul and body because it was only the fullness of life from God that was flowing through him. There was no sin, sickness, and disease anywhere on earth. Therefore, even his body would have lived forever. Note that the Holy Spirit didn't dwell in Adam, but Adam did not know sin. They knew God but the Holy Spirit did not dwell in their being. They were living in a time of innocence, meaning they had no knowledge of sin whatsoever. As a result, God could fellowship and walk and talk with Adam and Eve as friends. Adam's spirit was in relationship with God and this relationship ceased.

By rebelling against God and eating this forbidden fruit, Adam's spirit died and his soul was awakened to sin. Adam was suddenly developing his independence from God. Adam no longer had God's truth and life flowing through his spirit, because he chose to empower his soul with the nourishment from the fruit of the tree of knowledge of good and evil. That meant he would effectively manage his own life with his intellect, emotions, and his will. **Rebellion** and **independence from God** explain every sin committed.

Adam and Eve volitionally made a choice that they wanted to be like God and possess this knowledge of good and evil and take matters into their own hands, in other words be **independent from God**. But they are not God and did not have the capacity to properly manage this new level of knowledge without God's help. Satan gave them false hope that they could do it as good or better than God without Him. Adam soon began to realize his sin.

Adam's Body is Dying

Since Adam and Eve's spirit was not in communion with God, one major effect was that their soul began to rule their life and destiny with the wrong inputs instead of their previous God led spirit. In other words, some of the inputs (information and knowledge) to their soul were now being influenced by the devil, and some influenced by their own soulish perspectives or thoughts, and some from their sin-infected body and some from the world. To reiterate the point, Adam and Eve's souls began to rule their lives and they built their independent lives apart from God. They gave up their dependence on God.

> *This sin nature is passed to every one of Adam's descendants through his seed. Adam's seed incorporates or is identified with what we know today as DNA.*

As we discussed Adam and Eve's spirit was dead to God, but their flesh is awakened to sin. A physical effect of Adam's sin was that sin infected his body and he now had the nature of sin in his flesh. This sin nature also directly impacts their soul and spirit and will be passed from generation to future generations through man's seed (or DNA) not woman's seed. We will review this later in more detail, but the Bible tells us Satan is the father of sin and lies. And now sin is part of Adam's DNA. We are referring here to Adam the noun and as the representative of mankind.

So, while Adam's body did not die immediately, his body was subject to decay and would eventually die because of sin. Sickness and disease stand in between sin and death.

First sin comes and opens the door for sickness and disease, which then invites death. This is the chain of events that brings decay and death.

At this point in history God chose to limit man's physical life to approximately 850 to 1,000 years and his body will return to dust where it came from, and it will cease to exist in the same physical form.

We can see in our current physical state that at conception mankind's body begins to physically grow and develop. That seems to continue until about the age of thirty and we begin to see the process of devolution begin and eventually we physically die and return to dust. However, man's spirit and soul will not cease to exist. Adam and Eve's spirit and soul will continue to exist apart from God for eternity unless they are redeemed. Either way man's soul and spirit will go into eternity and will not wear out.

Adam lost his dominion over the earth

So, now we know that the world and all that is in it, was created by God and did not come from evolution. However, since the time of Adam's rebellion against God, and his inability to appropriately rule the world because of sin, the world has been experiencing a state of devolution. This includes man's physical body.

It's appropriate to recognize that Satan initiated this whole escapade in the garden to lure Adam into making this decision so that Satan could usurp Adam's dominion of the world. Nonetheless, in that decision Adam had chosen to rebel against God's command and he lost much of his God given dominion as the ruler of the world. Adam effectively forfeited his God given authority as ruler of the earth and Satan was ready to take advantage of it by usurping as much of Adam's authority as he could.

Lucifer was a created spirit being, a high-ranking angel that rebelled against God. After his rebellion, his name was changed to Satan. He is the one that introduced sin to Adam. Now, it is important to recognize that Adam had the authority to cast Satan out of the world, but instead Adam took the bait that Satan put in front of Adam, and Satan influenced Adam, creating confusion and doubts into Adam's soul. Satan's goal was to get Adam to release his God given authority over the world. God freely gave this authority to Adam and consequently Adam had the authority to give it to Satan. So, Adam originally had been given possession of the keys to authority over all the earth, but when he forfeited his innocence, he also gave up much of his authority.

Consequently, Adam allowed Satan to usurp this authority over the world. This opened the door for Satan to bring all the demons that followed him in his rebellion, to be released in the earth and they were allowed to bring all kinds of evil, sin, sickness, and death into the world.

Let's consider this in terms we use today. We know that God created the universe and as such He is the owner.

Psalms 24:1 (NKJV) The earth is the LORD's, and all its fullness, The world and those who dwell therein.

As the owner of all creation, God gave Adam a lease of the earth and everything in it. In this lease Adam is given dominion or authority over the earth. But when Adam ate the fruit of the tree of knowledge of good and evil, he was forfeiting his dominion of the earth to receive the knowledge of good and evil.

So, now we see that Adam's sin, first affected his being directly, but went beyond him into the rest of the world. The effect of Adam's sin was that he allowed his God given authority over the world to be usurped by Satan. As a result, sin was now allowed to flow throughout the world and all of God's creation was impacted including all the creatures and plants and the earth itself. Even the bodies of all other physical life on earth now had been exposed to sin and were feeding on these changes in the world, and its sin nature and filling their souls with knowledge of things pertaining to death or simply put "evil."

> *Jesus plainly told us that the devil comes to steal, kill, and destroy and this is exactly what was happening here. Satan purposed to steal Adam's dominion, kill him, and destroy him.*

God in His righteous and just nature has allowed changes in the world because of Adam's rebellion. **In His creation**, God had given Adam authority over all the earth. **In Adam's rebellion**, he chose death, forfeited his innocence, and released much of his authority to Satan.

An important point to establish here is that God owns and possesses all authority.

Colossians 1:16 (NKJV) [16] For by Him all things were created that are in heaven and that are on earth, visible and invisible, whether thrones or dominions or principalities or powers. All things were created through Him and for Him.

This scripture brings simple clarification that "*all things*" were created through Him and for Him. The reference to "*all things*" means just that, "*all things*" which includes all authority. Since all authority comes from God He can and does distribute authority. In this case He distributed authority over all the world to Adam. As we will discuss later it is important to understand details about authority. To properly manage the authority that God gave to Adam he needed to continue to be under God's authority or in other words **dependent** on God. As such I will repeat again Adam chose to be **independent** of God's authority. As a result of Adam's sin, he released much of his God given authority to Satan and Satan cleverly usurped this God given authority.

> *Romans 8:20-21 (NKJV) For the creation was subjected to futility, not willingly, but because of Him who subjected it in hope; [21] because the creation itself also will be delivered from the bondage of corruption into the glorious liberty of the children of God.*

This scripture is telling us that all of creation including the earth itself has experienced bondage from the devil's presence on the earth. We can see the devolution and destruction throughout all of creation around us and we can see this destruction has been growing at an accelerated pace. This destruction of the earth comes in many different forms such as earthquakes, hurricanes, tornadoes and the like. Similarly, the animal kingdom displays its destruction by devouring species that are weaker and death through sickness and disease. It's not just mankind but all of creation itself is aware of this destruction and looking forward to the return of Jesus Christ to bring redemption.

God's Redemption Plan Revealed and His Judgement Declared

We don't know exactly what Adam was thinking when he sinned, but scriptures do give us some insights.

> *Genesis 3:12 (NKJV)* ¹² *Then the man said, "The woman whom You gave to be with me, she gave me of the tree, and I ate."*

We will soon see that this is another mistake Adam made. Is Adam blaming God for giving him a wife? Is he blaming Eve, as if she made him eat the fruit? Or is Adam just trying to please Eve instead of following God because he loves her more than he loves God? What was he really thinking? Or was this just his way of making an excuse and not accepting responsibility?

> *1 Timothy 2:14 (NKJV)* ¹⁴ *And Adam was not **deceived**, but the woman being **deceived**, fell into transgression.*

As we discussed, we don't really know everything that Adam was thinking but we do know from this scripture that he wasn't deceived or perhaps we should say not deceived to the same degree as Eve. As mentioned earlier the word "deceived" is used twice in this verse. Some Bible scholars teach that the Greek use of this word refers to these in differing degrees of deception.

> *Genesis 3:17 (NKJV)* ¹⁷ *Then to Adam He said, "Because **you have heeded the voice of your wife**, and **have eaten from the tree** of which I commanded you, saying, 'You shall not eat of it'"......*

Most of us are aware that Adam rebelled by eating the forbidden fruit. But in this scripture, we see that God exposes and reveals that Adam committed two sins. The first was that he heeded to the voice of his wife **and** the second sin was that he ate the forbidden fruit. Now through this scripture we have some additional information about what Adam was thinking. Adam obviously loved Eve, his wife as he should have. We need to exercise caution as we review this because God is not saying that Adam's love for Eve was a sin. The mistake that Adam made was that he heeded to Eve's voice **instead** of the voice of God. As of the writing of this book I have been married almost forty years to the same woman. I would like to enjoy many more years with her so I will make it very clear – God is not upset because Adam adored his wife or that he wanted to please her. To the contrary, Adam's mistake was that he rebelled against God. Adam chose to disobey God and followed Eve's transgression which was rebellion against God.

God's plan for marriage is very clear. Man is the head of the household just as Jesus is the Head of the church. As the head of the household the husband should lead his wife and family to follow the leadership of God our Father. Jesus is the role model to husbands. We should listen to our wives, love them, cherish them, through thick and thin. Look at the suffering Jesus went through for His bride, the church. Remember Jesus is our role model, and we still put the name of Jesus above anyone's name. Jesus gave His life for us, but He would never disobey His Father to please His bride. That is a clear line that should never be crossed.

> *Genesis 3:23-24 (NKJV) therefore the LORD God sent him out of the garden of Eden to till the ground from which he was taken. [24] So He drove out the man; and He placed cherubim at the east of the garden of Eden, and a flaming sword which turned every way, to guard the way to the tree of life.*

Note that even though Adam disobeyed and rebelled against God's only command, God in His love and mercy, immediately began to implement man's protection and redemption plan. God ensures that Adam and Eve do not have access to the tree of life so that this status of "no communion" with God will not last forever. This is a clear indication that God plans to provide mankind another opportunity. God still loves Adam and Eve, and He still wants to have a loving relationship with them and all of mankind.

God's desire to fellowship with mankind has not changed, but because of God's righteousness, Adam's sin, and because He is a just God, He must execute justice. We are seeing part of God's character here. He cannot ignore their sin because He loves them. He told Adam and Eve they would die if they ate the fruit, and He had to keep His word and administer justice, but we will also see how He continues to release His love and grace to them.

Earlier we began to see the origin of the blame game. Adam blamed God for giving him Eve, and he blamed Eve for giving him the fruit. Eve, who was deceived, blamed the serpent for deceiving her. The blame game has continually been played routinely for the last 6,000 years. The blame game is similar to hide and seek. We saw the origins of that game when Adam and Eve tried to hide from God in the garden. Hide and seek is also still a popular game that mankind continues to play. But as we see, blaming others and trying to hide from sin has never worked. God in His righteous nature must execute judgement. After their sin is uncovered, God begins to unveil specifics to Adam, Eve, and the serpent, what is the impact and effect of their sin? His judgement is specific and directed to each one according to their specific role and responsibility. To the serpent He says;

> *Genesis 3:14-15 (NKJV) So the LORD God said to the serpent:*
> *"Because you have done this,*
> *You are cursed more than all cattle,*
> *And more than every beast of the field;*

On your belly you shall go,
*And **you shall eat dust***
All the days of your life.
[15] And I will put enmity
Between you and the woman,
And between your seed and her Seed;
He shall bruise your head,
And you shall bruise His heel."

God tells us about the devil's future and states that he is cursed more than all the cattle and more than any other beast in the field. This is a significant change from his original created status. When Lucifer was created and before his rebellion, we know he held a very high position of authority in heaven because he was a cherub angel. When Lucifer rebelled against God he was cast out of heaven and his name was changed to Satan. And now because of the deception he caused, he is being compared to and cursed more than the animals. Then God said, *"you shall eat dust all the days of your life."* There are other scriptures referring to this statement.

*Micah 7:17 (NKJV) [17] They shall **lick the dust like a serpent;***
They shall crawl from their holes like snakes of the earth.
They shall be afraid of the LORD our God,
And shall fear because of You.

Isaiah 65:25 (NKJV) [25] The wolf and the lamb shall feed together,
The lion shall eat straw like the ox,
*And **dust shall be the serpent's food.***
They shall not hurt nor destroy in all My holy mountain,"
Says the LORD.

These references to **eating the dust** highlight the humility intended for Satan. Satan is not to be exalted for his sin and rebellion, but rather we should be recognizing how humiliating it is to reject God and desire to be independent of God. It shows us that it is simply ignorance to not desire to be dependent on God.

Then God said, *"I will put enmity between you and the woman."* This essentially means there will be hatred and hostility between them. We know this will also include Eve's descendants because God follows up with *"and between your seed and her Seed."* Since Adam forfeited his authority, Satan and his demons now have access to influence the earth, the beasts of the earth, and mankind, as sin and death is spreading throughout the earth.

Then, God says that the Seed of the woman (Seed is referring to Jesus Christ) will crush Satan's head and that Satan will strike His heel. This is a symbolic statement prophesying the victory that comes from Jesus Christ's death, burial, and resurrection. Jesus Christ will then share the benefits of His victory (over sin, death, and the devil) with all of mankind who accept Him, believe, and trust in Him. Let us make no mistake, God (Elohim) is the creator of everything, and He is in charge and His plan will succeed or we can say with confidence "it has succeeded."

We will discuss in more detail later, but we see here that her Seed flows through to Jesus Christ. The reference to Satan's seed is referencing the seed of sin which is now part of Adam's DNA.

Then God said to Eve,

> *Genesis 3:16 (NKJV) "I will greatly multiply your sorrow*
> *and your conception;*
> *In pain you shall bring forth children;*
> *Your desire shall be for your husband,*
> *And he shall rule over you."*

As for Eve, her judgement falls on the woman's unique role of childbearing and her relationship with her husband. God says, *"will **greatly*** *multiply your sorrow and your conception."* Greatly multiplying is a significant statement. Sorrow and conception refer to the pregnancy and birth process. The changing hormones, morning sickness and many of the physical changes in a pregnant woman's body can make pregnancy difficult. And we are all aware of the significant pain that a woman experiences during childbirth.

Next God says that a woman's desire will be for her husband, and he shall rule over you. Many books have been written regarding this scripture and let's note this book is not a marriage training or counseling book. That said, this scripture does clarify God's structure of authority in the family. God is not implying that woman is lesser than Adam, but rather establishing that there needs to be a structure and recognition of the process of authority. Note this is one of many examples that not all of Adam's authority was usurped.

Then He said to Adam;

> *Genesis 3:17-19 (NKJV)* ¹⁷ *Then to Adam He said,*
> *"Because you have heeded the voice of your wife, and*
> *have eaten from the tree of which I commanded you,*
> *saying, 'You shall not eat of it'":*
> *"Cursed is the ground for your sake;*
> *In toil you shall eat of it*
> *All the days of your life.*
> ¹⁸ *Both thorns and thistles it shall bring forth for you,*
> *And you shall eat the herb of the field.*
> ¹⁹ *In the sweat of your face you shall eat bread*
>   *Till you return to the ground,*
> *For out of it you were taken;*
> *For dust you are,*
> *And to dust you shall return."*

God begins with Adam by clarifying or confirming what Adam's two sins were. Then He says, *"cursed is the ground for your sake."* It is clear there is a change in the relationship of man and the ground. We could say the relationship was now antagonistic as judgement fell on Adam's primary workplace and his source of food. *"In toil you shall eat of it all the days of your life."* This is a good place to note that this scripture was not the introduction of work and work itself was not the curse. In fact, in Genesis 2:15 it says God put Adam in the garden to tend and to keep it. This was before his sin. So, we can easily conclude that God always had planned for man to work. As such, we can recognize work as a blessing not a curse. What this scripture is saying is that the ground is cursed and therefore Adam's work will be more difficult to achieve, and the fruit of his labor may be more diminished than it was before his sin.

Then God says that Adam's body will die and return to the dust where it came from.

Adam's Nature Has Changed

To summarize the effect of Adam's sin in his being, his nature has now changed from the manner in which God created him. We are not just referring to the individual Adam, we are referring to Adam as representative of mankind. In other words, at this point of time in history all of mankind now has a different nature. Adam was created as a **spiritual man** in the image and likeness of God – without sin! His spirit was on the throne of his being and the goodness of God flowed through his being.

When Adam sinned, that sin became part of his DNA. The sin in his body stimulates fleshly desires and his soul now submits to these desires instead of his spirit. Adam's spirit is more passive as the self of the soul aligns with the desires in the body. The Bible refers to this new alignment as the **fleshly man**. As we discussed, the soul of man is "you." Your soul, which is your mind, emotions and will has transferred its allegiance which was to his spirit and now his soul supports the body of sin. Adam was created with his spirit on the throne and now his flesh is on the throne.

Now, part of Adam's nature is sin. We can say Adam has a sin nature. And again, this describes all of mankind. This sin nature is part of Adam's genes and is passed down to every generation through the man (male). It is his seed that carries sin, and it affects every child born, both male and female.

Additionally, Satan and his minions have captured much authority on the earth. Consequently, sin, sickness, hatred, death, and all kinds of evil roam the earth to kill, steal, and destroy God's creation.

CHAPTER 5

Perspective on Sin

What is Sin and Its Nature?

People around the world today have many different perspectives on sin, some try to justify their sin, some ignore their sin as if it did not exist, and some try to redefine the scope of sin. But sadly, many do not use the Bible as their source to understand sin. None of the opinions of people will change what sin is or the impact it has on them. In this chapter we will take a closer look at what the Bible says about sin and the nature of sin.

A simple definition is that all sin creates desire for man to miss the mark that God has planned for him and destroy man's relationship with God by keeping man separated from God. Sin purposes to grasp our attention and distract us from fellowship with God.

Sin separates us from God because God is holy, and He will not dwell with sin. Therefore, we can conclude that if we have sin we cannot fellowship with God. Sin has its own nature, and its purpose is to separate us from God. Sin is never satisfied; it feeds on itself and wants to grow and take over.

> *Proverbs 27:20 (NKJV)* [20] *Hell and Destruction are never full;*
> *So the eyes of man are never satisfied*

Sin also has many demonic friends, such as Hell, Destruction, and Death. To explain this scripture there is not a waiting list to enter hell. There is room for all that are condemned to death and hell for eternity. *"So, the eyes of man are never satisfied"* is referring to man's focus and intents being towards sin. His sin or sin nature never gets enough and continues its desire in man.

> *Habakkuk 2:5 (NKJV)* [5] *"Indeed, because he transgresses by wine",*
> *He is a proud man,*
> *And he does not stay at home.*
> *Because he enlarges his desire as hell,*
> ***And he is like death, and cannot be satisfied,***
> *He gathers to himself all nations*
> *And heaps up for himself all peoples.*

This scripture is similar in that it shows how sin, death, and hell are never satisfied. All we must do is look at the effects from our culture in our society to see the effects of this truth. How many people are addicted to alcohol, drugs, pornography, pride, bitterness, hatred, gossip, greed, lust, and other sinful habits? These addictions are clear and easy to see how their desire is to consume mankind into destruction, death and hell through sin and it is never satisfied, it always wants more. Once the door is opened, the desires of our flesh, the desire to sin is more and more compelling. Man becomes blinded and eventually only sees his desire for his sin.

The nature and purpose of sin is to bring destruction and death. Sin is deceiving, and its desire is to separate you from God.

> *Genesis 4:7 (NKJV)* [7] *If you do well, will you not be accepted? And if you do not do well, **sin lies at the door**. And its desire is for you, but you should rule over it."*

In this scripture God is speaking to Cain before he killed his brother Able. God is encouraging Cain to do well. Cain already missed the mark with his sacrifice and Cain is likely already considering whether he should kill his brother Able, because he is angry and jealous that God accepted Abel's sacrifice and not his. So, God is warning Cain about his thoughts.

"*Sin lies at the door*", means that sin is waiting for you to release the opportunity for it to take advantage of you. Some translations use the term crouching over its prey. But sin can't leap onto its prey unless you release the trigger and give it permission.

God is also encouraging Cain and telling him that he can overcome his sinful desires, and he can rule over sin. God is simply describing how we should be managing our thoughts. Sin is waiting for you to open the door. Its desire is for you. Sin is not slothful, and it is persistent. Sin wants to occupy your thoughts, and if you allow it to occupy just a little bit, then sin gets into your imagination. Then after dwelling in your imagination, it sinks into your heart and becomes an intention.

When sin gets into your heart, it will begin to flow out of your mouth through your words.

> *Luke 6:45 (NKJV)* [45] *A good man out of the good treasure of his heart brings forth good; and an evil man out of the evil treasure of his heart brings forth evil. For out of the abundance of the heart his mouth speaks.*

The very words that come out of our mouth reveal what is in our heart. God was encouraging Cain to do good, because out of the abundance of the heart can come good or evil. What is in abundance in your heart? Is it good or evil? Frequently the Bible refers to thoughts as trees. Trees produce fruit and so do thoughts.

Luke 6:43-44 (NKJV) For a good tree does not bear bad fruit, nor does a bad tree bear good fruit. ⁴⁴ For every tree is known by its own fruit. For men do not gather figs from thorns, nor do they gather grapes from a bramble bush.

The relationship between trees and thoughts are very clear. What kind of fruit are your thoughts producing? I have found that most people are not aware of the thought trees they are growing. This is how sin works. It seems very subtle – after all it's only a thought – right? But each thought tree can grow and bear fruit. We can discern what that fruit is when we speak because our words are a display of what is in our heart. So, it starts with how we think and then it becomes the words we speak and eventually the deeds that we do.

We were all born with a sin nature and therefore sinful thoughts do come into our minds. And the nature of sin is to take over, much like a field that is growing crops. Our enemy, the adversary or the devil also sows seeds of evil or like weeds. Both good thoughts and evil thoughts come, and the Bible tells us that we have authority over our thoughts. We have total control over the thoughts we choose to dwell on and how we dwell on each thought. It therefore is important that we maintain an awareness of our thoughts and take them captive. We then need to follow up by insisting in our own minds that we think the correct thoughts.

Philippians 4:8-9 (NKJV) Finally, brethren, whatever things are true, whatever things are noble, whatever things are just, whatever things are pure, whatever things are lovely, whatever things are of good report, if there is any virtue and if there is anything praiseworthy—meditate on these things. ⁹ The things which you learned and received and heard and saw in me, these do, and the God of peace will be with you.

So, if we think about these things that the Bible tells us to think about, we will begin talking and walking in the Spirit rather than talking and walking in the ways of this world.

Sin is powerful, and desires to consume you. It only has the authority that we give to it.

We also see in this scripture that we have authority over sin. It says we should rule over it. That means we have the choice. This is a continual battle, and we can't expect sin to go away just because we ignore it. We must purpose to win the battle over sin by continually and purposely thinking the way the Bible tells us to think.

What is the Origin of Sin?

As we look at sin, we should begin by looking at the origin and history of sin. The first sin recorded in the Bible was of Lucifer. Lucifer was a created Cherub angel. We can see in the scriptures that he was created as a beautiful being. He was filled with wisdom and anointed by God. At least until iniquity was found in him.

> *Ezekiel 28:11-15 (NKJV) Moreover the word of the LORD came to me, saying,* ¹² *"Son of man, take up a lamentation for the king of Tyre, and say to him," 'Thus says the Lord GOD:*
> *"You were the seal of perfection,"*
> *Full of wisdom and perfect in beauty.*
> ¹³ *You were in Eden, the garden of God;*
> *Every precious stone was your covering:*
> *The sardius, topaz, and diamond,*
> *Beryl, onyx, and jasper,*
> *Sapphire, turquoise, and emerald with gold.*
> *The workmanship of your timbrels and pipes*
> *Was prepared for you on the day you were created.*

[14] *"You were the anointed cherub who covers;"*
I established you;
You were on the holy mountain of God;
You walked back and forth in the midst of fiery stones.
[15] You were perfect in your ways from the day you were created,
Till iniquity was found in you.

As a background, at the beginning of this chapter 28:1, Ezekiel is prophesying to the **prince** of Tyre. Now, in verse eleven he is referring to the **king** of Tyre. Many Bible scholars bring clarification that the prince is the physical man in charge and Satan himself is the king who has set up a spiritual throne over Tyre and Satan directs the prince.

Beginning in verse one God tells Ezekiel to tell the prince that because of his great success he began to think of himself as a god. So, he accrued massive wealth for this nation, and he began to think of himself as a god. Pride was in him, and he thought his greatness was because of all he did by himself, so he self-declared himself as a god.

But Ezekiel goes on and prophecies and says – no you are but a man and you are filled with pride. He then goes on to say that other nations will come against him, and he will be killed and thrown into the Pit.

Now in verse eleven the Lord continues to speak to Ezekiel, but he switches from the prince to the king; it appears God is relating the pride of the king of Tyre to the pride and sin of Lucifer, because He shifted from talking about the king to talking about Lucifer.

The end of verse 13 says that God created Lucifer. We see that he was created with wisdom and beauty. And we see that musical instruments (timbrels and pipes) were created for him. He was a master musician, and perfect in all his ways because that was how God created him. The king of Tyre was like Lucifer in that he allowed pride to enter in and iniquity was found in him.

We see in verse fifteen that Lucifer was perfect in all his ways until iniquity was found in him. It then goes on to say that he defiled his sanctuaries by the multitude of his iniquities. We see the nature of sin right away. Sin multiplied and consumed Satan quickly, and as sin devoured him and he became a horror to people.

We can also see the prophet Isaiah speaking the words God that spoke through him about Lucifer as well.

> *Isaiah 14:12-14 (NKJV)* [12] *"How you are fallen from heaven,*
> *O Lucifer, son of the morning!"*
> *How you are cut down to the ground,*
> *You who weakened the nations!*
> [13] *For you have said in your heart:*
> *I will ascend into heaven,*
> *I will exalt my throne above the stars of God;*
> *I will also sit on the mount of the congregation*
> *On the farthest sides of the north;*
> [14] *I will ascend above the heights of the clouds,*
> *I will be like the Most High.'*

God spoke through the prophet Isaiah in a similar format as He did to Ezekiel.

Isaiah tells us how the pride of Lucifer came to be. Lucifer spoke in his heart. It does not say that he vocalized it. This gives us a clue that his pride began as a thought. He began recognizing how wonderful He was. The truth is, and the Word confirms, that Lucifer was wonderful. For Lucifer to recognize it was not the problem. The key point is that God made him that way. In other words, Lucifer was not wonderful because of what he did – he was wonderful because God made him that way. He should have been thanking God for making him that way, but when Lucifer focused on himself, His focus was not on God it was on himself. He became self-conscious instead of God-conscious. Another view is that Lucifer gave up his **dependence** on God and became **independent** of God.

He said *"I will ascend into heaven; I will exalt my throne above the stars of God…. I will be like the Most High"*. Thoughts can become desires and desires can grow and manifest into sin. This is what happened to Lucifer. He became greater and greater in his own eyes. He thought he could be just like God. His thoughts grew into desire, and desire grew into sin. Then his sin of pride grabbed hold of him and continued to grow into other sins, like jealousy, greed, bitterness, and so on. So, now we know that sin originated in Lucifer, and he was cast out of God's presence. We also know that one-third of the angels in heaven followed Satan when he was cast out of heaven. As a result, they are now called demons rather than angels. Their decision to follow Satan, now puts Satan and his demon followers in a different category that is different from the other two-thirds of angels that remained loyal to God and dependent on God.

We can see from both Ezekiel and in Isiah that pride was the root that developed in Satan's heart. He foolishly thought he could be equal to or above God. It is the same anchor that Satan used when he tempted Adam and Eve and pulled them down. He told them they could be just like God and consequently they could be **independent of God**.

As we summarize this situation with Lucifer, he was created by God with wonderful beauty with the intent he would live in a high position of authority in God's Kingdom. Lucifer brought sin into his being and as a result was cast out of God's presence (became dead to God). We know that God will not dwell with sin, which is why he was cast out of God's presence and out of God's Kingdom.

Iniquity originated in Satan, and as his iniquities multiplied, because that is the nature of sin. Sin is never satisfied, and it wants to consume. Iniquity is sin but denotes a concept of direct rebellion rather than passive sin. As Satan's iniquities multiplied, sin became his nature. Satan's nature is now sin and death.

Then sometime after Satan's fall, God created Adam, who was a different type of creature, a human being. As a human being he was also created with wonderful beauty, and he was given authority to rule the earth with the intent he would also live for eternity in this capacity under the authority of God.

We see then how Satan's sin of pride begins to grow into other sins like jealousy. Satan is jealous of the newly created man called Adam, and the fact that this new guy called Adam, was given authority over the whole earth. So, Satan sneaks in as a snake and deceives Adam and Eve to usurp as much of their authority as he can. Satan understood both his and mankind's freedom of choice and he also understood the power of pride. He also knew he had to be sneaky and deceiving in stealing any authority from Adam. Remember God gave Adam authority over the earth and that authority belonged to Adam. That meant that Satan could not just come in and steal authority directly from Adam because it belonged to Adam. Satan had to find a way to get Adam to let go of his authority, or in other words, to release his authority to Satan.

We now know the next part of the story that God in His infinite wisdom, authority, and compassion for mankind has already developed and planned for the implementation of mankind's salvation from sin. Jesus declared the motive of both sides in this next scripture.

> *John 10:10 (NKJV)* *¹⁰ The thief does not come except to steal, and to kill, and to destroy. I have come that they may have life, and that they may have it more abundantly.*

It's interesting to note the phrase "the thief does not come except". This implies the only reason Satan came to earth was to steal, kill, and destroy. Satan is the thief, and now we can clearly see his purpose was to come and steal Adam's authority, to kill him, and destroy Adam as the representative of mankind, and any of God's creation that he can. Since then, Satan has not changed – his purpose is still the same but now his target is not the man named Adam it is you, me, and all of mankind.

> The contrast of **purpose and intent** is vividly clear; "the thief only comes to steal, kill, and destroy." "Jesus came to give life and that we will have life more abundantly."

We can also clearly see Jesus's purpose of coming and He does not sneak in, He comes in legally and directly in the front door. Jesus comes in humility; He left His throne as the King of kings to humble Himself to enter this world as a man so that He could provide a means for mankind to return to Him in a full loving relationship. A loving relationship that is filled with an abundance of life – the "zoe" life.

As we speak of authority it is important to state again that all authority is God's, and He will always oversee all authority.

That said, there are examples in the Bible where God gives various levels or types of authority to individuals. Authority is a gift that needs to be managed and we are to be good stewards of the authority we have been given. As in the case of Adam as the representative of mankind, his authority could be given away or passed on to another because God gave Adam the legal rights to that authority.

We read in Genesis 25:27-34 another example of authority being usurped when the twins Esau and Jacob were born. Esau was the first-born which entitled him to certain benefits including the blessing from Isaac their father. Jacob deceived Esau and Isaac his father, so that he could receive this blessing from Isaac which was an irrevocable blessing. In the natural order that God provided the blessing, it belonged to Esau, but Jacob usurped it from him. In a similar manner Jacob had to figure out a way to get Esau to release his authority to him. Jacob waited for the right opportunity when Esau was weak. Just like with Adam, Esau later regretted that he gave up his birthright, but it was too late to take it back.

Father of Sin

It is important to understand the role of a father and to recognize and choose who your father is. In John chapter eight, Jesus is teaching in the temple. The Pharisees are asking Jesus where He came from, and Jesus begins to talk about His Father, and He describes the relationship He has with His Father.

> John 8:28-29 (NKJV) Then Jesus said to them, "When you lift up the Son of Man, then you will know that I am He, and that I do nothing of Myself; but as My Father taught Me, I speak these things. [29] And He who sent Me is with Me. The Father has not left Me alone, for I always do those things that please Him."

This is a beautiful picture of the Father and Son relationship. Jesus is speaking here as the Son of Man, which is referring to Himself as a man not as the Son of God. The Father instructs His Son, and He is always present with His Son. On the other hand, the Son learns from His Father, and clings to His Father and always desires to do those things that please His Father. Now, we have some awareness of the nature and origin of sin. As such, since Satan is the originator of sin and it is the core part of his nature, it should be no surprise that the Bible refers to Satan as the blue father of sin.

> The nature of a father is replicated in his descendants. His children naturally follow the lead of their father.

> *John 8:37-38 (NKJV) "I know that you are Abraham's descendants, but you seek to kill Me, because My word has no place in you. ³⁸ I speak what I have seen with My Father, and you do what you have seen with your father."*

In this scripture Jesus is speaking to a group of Jewish men, the Pharisees. He had just told them in prior scripture that if they believed in Him as Messiah, they could be set free from sin. They responded to Jesus by stating they were sons of Abraham, believing that should make them qualified to be accepted into God's Kingdom. Jesus acknowledged they were sons of Abraham in the flesh, but they didn't believe and trust in Jesus as their Savior in the same manner that Abraham did. These men knew from Old Testament scriptures that they were descendants of Abraham and that God said Abraham was a righteous man. They were focused on their relationship to Abraham's fleshly nature and not perceiving Abraham's spiritual nature. Then Jesus clarifies here the difference between Jesus' Father and their father which is Satan.

> *John 8:44 (NKJV) ⁴⁴ You are of your father the devil, and the desires of your father you want to do. He was a murderer from the beginning, and does not stand in the truth, because there is no truth in him. When he speaks a lie, he speaks from **his own resources**, for he is a liar and the father of it.*

Jesus continues telling these men that their spiritual father is the devil, and their desire is to follow their spiritual father. Their father, the devil, is a murderer and a liar. Satan lied to Adam and Eve and initiated their death. He goes on to say that Satan is a liar and speaks from **his own resources** and he is the father of lies.

Remember in Genesis chapter three God spoke of the Seed of Eve which is pointing to Jesus Christ and as God impregnated Mary, it clearly establishes God as the Father of Jesus just as Jesus correctly proclaimed. Joseph was the adoptive father of Jesus and consequently the earthly father of Jesus, so the fleshly seed of sin was not transferred into Jesus' being.

Genesis chapter three also referred to Satan's seed which is sin that became part of Adam's DNA. That fleshly seed was transferred through the generations to Abraham's flesh or DNA and is still continuing to be transferred to every person born. This explains how Satan has become their father. Satan's seed is part of their flesh, and they are choosing to follow Satan, instead of Jesus as the Son of man and the Son of God the Father.

It can be helpful to stop and recognize what sin is and that it comes from the devil who is our enemy. Just having awareness of that can help us to hate sin and seek shelter from Jesus Christ our Lord. In other words, we should be like Jesus to be **dependent** on God the Father in every part of our lives.

Process and Development of Sin

> *At first glance sin often appears desirable. It appears as a friend wanting to make you feel good. But its intent is to steal, kill, and destroy you.*

The scriptures above reveal the root source of sin, which is Satan. And it tells us that they (Pharisees) want to do the desires of their father the devil. So, we know that the root source of sin is the devil.

James 1:14-15 (NKJV) ⁴ But each one is tempted when he is drawn away by his own desires and enticed. ¹⁵ Then, when desire has conceived, it gives birth to sin; and sin, when it is full-grown, brings forth death.

James brings some clarity to the process of sin. First, recognize a source of temptation comes as we are drawn away by our own fleshly desires. "*Drawn away*" is referring to being drawn away or separated from God's presence. A desire is a craving or longing for something. It is generally a term used for something forbidden like lust, particularly if it is coming from our flesh which possesses the very nature of sin. After a man is drawn away by his desires he is enticed. This word enticed means bait or to catch with bait. So, if we take the bait, desire then conceives and then gives birth to sin.

So, if we are drawn away by our own desires, perhaps we can look at the source of our desires. Where do our desires come from?

> *Ephesians 2:2-3 (NKJV) in which you once walked according to the course of this world, according to the prince of the power of the air, the spirit who now works in the sons of disobedience, ³ among whom also we all once conducted ourselves in the lusts of our flesh, fulfilling the desires of the flesh and of the mind, and were by nature children of wrath, just as the others.*

This scripture gives us some insight. Verse 2 tells us that Satan is busy influencing those walking according to the course of this world. Then in verse 3 Paul is saying, there is lust in our flesh, and we can fulfill the **desires** of our flesh and of the mind. The desire of our mind refers to our thoughts. In other words, if we are thinking about these desires or contemplating them even though we have not acted on them yet, it can be sin or lead us into sin. We have authority over our thoughts and can choose to continue dwelling on a thought until it becomes sin, or we can take that thought captive and pursue Godly thoughts.

We can see this as a process.

1. First, as sinners we walk according to the course or ways of this world.

2. That leaves us vulnerable to the influences of sin and Satan.

3. The lust of our flesh is ignited.

4. We begin fulfilling the desires of our flesh and mind.

So, it starts by being in the wrong place – "walking according to the course of this world." This is optional if we are born-again, or we can also choose to walk according to the spirit. If we are not walking with the world, we reduce the amount of influence the devil has in our life. While we do still live in this world we don't need to dwell in the center of sin. This is not difficult to recognize if we open our eyes.

> How would your life change if you gave Jesus full control of your viewing habits on TV, computer, or smart phone?

It may be that we need to consider the friends we have. Do they encourage godly behavior or sinful behavior? Another significant example would be what we watch on television, computer, or smartphone. It is easy to justify what we watch but what if you took it to another level? What if Jesus was always with you and you allowed Him to be in control of your remote or keypad, mouse? Which tv shows would you be watching, videos or searches on the internet? Would Jesus turn on the same shows, or videos or internet searches that you do? So, the first key to avoid the influence of the devil is to constantly be analyzing our lifestyles.

Matthew 5:28 (NKJV) ²⁸ But I say to you that whoever looks at a woman to lust for her has already committed adultery with her in his heart.

Jesus makes it clear in this scripture that sin can begin with our thoughts. He says if a man looks at a woman in lust, he has already committed adultery. Jesus is referring to a man's thoughts or the way he thinks. This sinful thought process is not restricted to lust and immorality. Jesus is giving us a warning that we should be careful to manage our thoughts effectively because they can lead us into sin.

> *Matthew 5:22 (NKJV) ²² But I say to you that whoever is angry with his brother without a cause shall be in danger of the judgment. And whoever says to his brother, Raca!' shall be in danger of the council. But whoever says, 'You fool!' shall be in danger of hell fire.*

To reiterate this reference to our thoughts let us consider this scripture. Jesus is showing us again to be careful about how we manage our thoughts. He is giving us a clear warning that if we dwell on the anger, we have towards our brother is a very dangerous position to maintain. It can lead us into bitterness which opens the gates to a further development of sin.

Let us look at Peter's advice in this next scripture.

> *1 Peter 5:8 (NKJV) ⁸ Be sober, be vigilant; because your adversary the devil walks about like a roaring lion, seeking whom he may devour.*

Another key point to recognize is that Peter is warning us here that Satan is our adversary. An adversary is an opponent and this opponent, the devil walks about like a roaring lion. I have been told that when a lion is hunting, the lion hides until he sees his prey and roars very loud. His prey hears the loud roar and in fear runs away quickly. The lion has his lionesses already positioned in the distance. He expects his prey to run away, and his prey is unaware that they are running right into the lionesses to be caught and killed. Peter is telling us to be sober or on guard so that we don't fall into traps like this and get lured into falling into sin.

> *Luke 10:18-20 (NKJV) [18] And He said to them, "I saw Satan fall like lightning from heaven. [19] Behold, I give you the authority to trample on serpents and scorpions, and over all the power of the enemy, and nothing shall by any means hurt you. [20] Nevertheless do not rejoice in this, that the spirits are subject to you, but rather rejoice because your names are written in heaven."*

We see here that Jesus has given us (the Church) authority over all the power of the enemy. We will talk more about Jesus' victory at His death and resurrection later. But it is important to note that Satan and all demons do not have control or power over us and our thoughts unless we give it away to them. Satan is bitter and jealous because he knows his destiny. While the fact that Jesus has given us this authority is a significant benefit to us as born-again human beings, Jesus tells us that this is not what we should be rejoicing in. Earlier we discussed that the main thing was **life** and **death**, and we should choose life. Jesus is confirming that point in this scripture. He said we should be rejoicing that our name is written in heaven (which is referring to life). This helps us to stay grounded and major on the majors. Let us keep the main thing at the center of all that we do. Remember Adam had authority to stop Satan from his pursuit, but he yielded that authority to Satan. We also saw that God showed Cain that he had the authority over sin, but he still chose to kill his brother Able. Now today we are in a comparable situation because we also have authority over sin and Satan. Jesus granted that authority to us.

Sin, Trespass, Transgression, and Iniquity – What is the Difference?

These four terms seem to be used interchangeably at times, but they do in fact have different meanings.

> *Psalms 32:5 (NKJV)* ⁵ *I acknowledged my* **sin** *to You,*
> *And my* **iniquity** *I have not hidden.*
> *I said, "I will confess my* **transgressions** *to the LORD,"*
> *And You forgave the* **iniquity** *of my* **sin***.*
> *Selah*

The simple fact that we see three of these words sin, transgression, and iniquity used in verse five should cause us to recognize that these words each have a different connotation. As I have studied these terms, I have found them difficult to separate and clarify. With that said many individuals have taught these words and I have consolidated my understanding of the differences.

1. **Sin** - The word sin is a more general term that denotes, to miss the mark. It is likened to an archer aiming at a target. Every time a person performs an action which violates a law of God that person has missed the mark. Perhaps an individual was not aware that they were violating an established command of God, it doesn't matter, they still sinned and missed His mark. Sin is a broad and general term that can incorporate trespass, transgression, and iniquity. Sin, as stated in Romans 3:23 is a general term used for anything that *"falls short of the glory of God"*. We sin because we are born sinners, with the sin nature of Adam (mankind). Sin can be further defined as any thought, word, or action that conveys or displays something or someone to be more valuable than Jesus, because sin is generated from three desires — the

lust of the eyes, the lust of the flesh and the pride of life. 1 John 2:15-17.

1 John 3:4 (NKJV) [4] *Whoever commits sin also commits lawlessness, and sin is lawlessness.*

John uses different words to describe sin but still brings us to the same conclusion.

2. **Trespass** refers to crossing a line that a person should not cross. A trespass may be intentional or unintentional. A property owner may post a sign saying, "no trespassing." That means the owner of the property does not want you to cross the line to their property. It can relate to sin through the law by showing the line that God has established between right and wrong. If we cross that line, we are trespassing, whether we are aware of it or not.

3. **Transgression** is rebelling against God. It means an individual is aware that an action is against God's law but still chooses to disobey; to willfully trespass or cross the line. When we knowingly do wrong, for example, to run a stop sign, tell a lie, or blatantly disregard an authority, we are transgressing. I John 3:4 – *for sin is the transgression of the law.* This is clear that all sin is rebellion against God's law.

4. **Iniquity** is a premeditated choice to sin and continue without repentance. Iniquity also tends to carry an emphasis towards perversity. To "sin" points to an action taken, perhaps without knowing or by accident, whereas a transgression denotes the conduct of a person who chooses to do wrong when they know the right way to walk. A transgressor "chooses" to do wrong. Iniquity seems to include the next step beyond transgression when an individual not only proposes to ignore God's law in order to fulfill a desire but also proposes to just go against God and then justify his actions.

When any of these four terms are used in the Bible their definition confirms that continual thoughts or actions related to these words can separate us from God.

Fortunately for us God is a holy God, and He is consistently holy and has been and will be holy throughout eternity. That is a key component of His character, and we are made in His image. To be holy indicates that we are separated from sin – set apart from sin. When Adam sinned, he essentially invited sin into the world. And now sin is running rampant throughout the world. As born-again believers we don't have to walk according to the ways of the world, even though we live in the world we can be holy or set apart (separated) from the sins of the world. It is a choice we make every day.

In summary we can recognize that the entry point of sin in mankind was through his body when Adam and Eve ate the fruit from the tree of knowledge of good and evil. While sin entered man's being through his physical body it was his soul that made the decision to allow it to happen. It was his "will" which is the part of his soul that decided to commit his desire and allegiance away from God and be independent from God. This decision was a volitional act that grabbed hold of his complete soul including his emotions and intellect or reasoning.

Consequently, sin infected his whole being and caused his spirit to die or in other words caused a disconnection from his spiritual life source, which was God. In essence Adam was telling God that he wanted his independence from God and God had to allow Adam to make that choice. The fruit from the tree of knowledge of good and evil introduced a seed called sin in Adam.

> *Man's soul and body joined together, and the alliance of the soul and desires of the body is generally referred to as his **flesh**.*

CHAPTER 6

Perspective on the Law

What is the Law?

Law is a very simple three letter word that has a deep and broad range of meanings. Merriam Webster dictionary gives several synonyms, law, rule, regulation, precept, statute, and ordinance, and all these words can refer to - **a principle governing action or procedure**. While each of these synonyms are closely related, they each have their own distinct meaning, and all are closely related to law.

The Bible has many different references to laws such as the law of faith – Romans 3:27, the royal law – James 2:8 just to name a few. Another simple law that God established is the law of gravity. While the law of gravity may not be specifically referenced in the Bible it is a law and was clearly established by God during His creation.

> *Romans 7:25 (NKJV)* [25] *I thank God—through Jesus Christ our Lord!*
> *So then, with the mind I myself serve the law of God, but with the flesh the law of sin.*

In this scripture Paul is saying that with his mind, which is referring to himself or his soul he serves the *"Law of God,"* and then he immediately follows up by saying that his flesh serves the *"law of sin."*

This can seem very confusing but as we break this down it becomes simple. Paul is relating the law of God - to his mind, and the law of sin - to his flesh. We just described the flesh as an alliance of the {soul and the body). Our mind is part of our soul. So Paul is comparing this alliance or the flesh to the mind which is a part of the soul.

These references are cited, primarily to establish how broad "law" can be. There are many laws in the Bible, and it is good to understand the purpose of the laws that God provided to mankind.

> *Romans 8:2 (NKJV) ² For the law of the Spirit of life in Christ Jesus has made me free from the **law of sin and death**.*

We start with the question, what is the law of sin and death? We know this answer from the beginning of Genesis. Adam sinned and he died, it is that simple. The Bible is clear on this subject; sin brings death. When Adam ate the forbidden fruit, he knew that it was opposing God's will, because God gave Adam very specific instructions.

But what if man does not understand what sin is? Can he plead ignorance and obtain a free pass, and get away with sin? What does the Bible say about that? Let's look at the effect of sin on mankind before the Mosaic law was given to man.

> *Romans 5:13-14 (NKJV) (For until the law sin was in the world, but sin is not imputed when there is no law. ¹⁴ Nevertheless death reigned from Adam to Moses, even over those who had not sinned according to the likeness of the transgression of Adam, who is a type of Him who was to come.*

This scripture makes it simple. Before the law, man could not specify or identify specific sins. In other words, people didn't say, he committed adultery, or he lied to me, or he stole this from me. It says, *"but sin is not imputed."* Imputed means to reckon in, or set to one's account, or apply to one's charge. In other words, there was not a list of sins that were charged against a person. The issue was that every person had a sin nature and every person sinned. It was more of a yes or no type of situation and the answer was always yes, man did have a sin nature and that allowed death to reign over mankind. So, as this scripture states, because of sin, death reigned from the time of Adam's judgement to the time when Moses introduced the law. Before Moses the only specific sin that could be imputed or identified were the transgressions or the sins of Adam that were identified.

> *Romans 7:7 (ESV)* *⁷ What then shall we say? That the law is sin? By no means! Yet if it had not been for the law, I would not have known sin. For I would not have known what it is to covet if the law had not said, "You shall not covet."*

So, we see here that it was the law that brought sin to our awareness and provided a means to identify sin. But prior to Moses they didn't have the law. Let's see what happened before the law was introduced by Moses.

> *Genesis 6:5 (NKJV)* *⁵ Then the LORD saw that the **wickedness of man** was great in the earth, and that every intent of the thoughts of his heart was only evil continually.*

We see that after Adam's sin the **wickedness of mankind** continued to grow because that is the nature of sin. Even though they were not aware of the specifics of their sins, their minds and hearts were focused on evil continually.

> *Genesis 6:11-12 (NKJV) The **earth also was corrupt** before God, and the earth was filled with violence. ¹² So*

God looked upon the earth, and indeed it was corrupt; for all flesh had corrupted their way on the earth.

We also see another effect of Adam's sin is that the **earth was corrupted**. Sin had not only infiltrated mankind but continued to corrupt all other flesh. Even the animal kingdom eventually began turning on each other and killing each other because the earth was filled with violence. As we noted in the last chapter, sin and death are never satisfied. All of life on earth was spiraling into death. God had to intervene and slow the process of devolution.

> *Genesis 6:8-9 (NKJV) But Noah found grace in the eyes of the LORD.*
> *⁹ This is the genealogy of Noah. Noah was a just man, perfect in his generations. Noah walked with God.*

God recognized the severity and depth of the evil that sin brought into the world.

> *God knew He had to implement judgement on mankind and the earth to preserve mankind and the earth.*

Noah was a type and shadow of the Savior that was to come, Jesus Christ. We all know the story of how Noah believed God and built the ark to bring salvation from the flood or judgement on earth to the animals and mankind.

We can summarize and reach three conclusions about sin and death during this time in the history of mankind.

1. First, even though man didn't have full knowledge about sin and didn't fully understand sin, sin still had its way in mankind and throughout the earth and brought forth death. Therefore, we also know that ignorance is not an acceptable plea for the person that

sins. In other words, that person that sins is still judged, and declared guilty, and sentenced to death.

2. The second conclusion is that there was still a means of salvation. *"Noah found grace in the eyes of the Lord."* Noah believed in the Lord. There were also others before Noah that walked with God. His family also believed, and they were also saved. This is a confirmation that at that time man still had a choice of life or death.

3. Now if we combine the first two conclusions, we can also affirm that mankind inherently knows the difference between right and wrong. Noah had purposed in his heart to believe God and he was saved. Like Adam, the others on this day chose death.

Now after the flood God blessed Noah and his three sons and said, *"be fruitful and multiply and fill the earth."* As the population grows, we continue reading in Genesis, and we see the sinful nature in man is still prevalent in the earth, and that it is still negatively affecting mankind. But we also can see how God's complete plan for redemption is still being unveiled. Let's look at the next big step in His plan and how we got the Mosaic law and how it affected mankind.

How and Why Did God Give Us the Law?

As we traverse through a brief history lesson to show how we received the law, let's also consider an even more important perspective, which is, why did God give His law to us. In the Old Testament we read that God had picked Israel to be His chosen people, set apart to be His example to the nations of the world. How and why did the nation of Israel begin?

It Started With Abraham

It started when God called Abraham to leave a land filled with idolatry and cultic activity. By faith Abraham believed and he obeyed God and traveled to the land that would become known as the nation of Israel. This land was promised by God to Abraham through his descendants. God brought him into the land of the Canaanites which at the time was also filled and dominated with sin and idolatry. But God had plans for that to change through the Israelites. So why did God choose Abraham to lead this movement and what was significant about Abraham?

> *Genesis 18:19 (Voice) 19 I have chosen him for a reason, namely that he will carefully instruct his children and his household to keep themselves strong in relationship to Me and to walk in My ways by doing what is good and right in the world and by showing mercy and justice to all others. I know he will uphold his end of the covenant, so that he can ensure My promises to him will be fulfilled and upheld as well.*

This verse highlights leadership traits of a loving father that are important to God.

God chose Abraham because he believed God and he obeyed God. As a result, we see several leadership traits displayed through him. God had confidence in Abraham that he would train his descendants and servants to establish and maintain their relationship with God and walk in His ways. This is a beautiful portrait of Abraham's role as the physical father of the Israelites. If the Israelites were going to be an example to other nations and ultimately be an example to the peoples of the world in the ways of God, they needed to be trained effectively. God blessed Abraham with leadership skills that continued to be implemented throughout the generations.

Abraham, whom we also have known as the father of our faith, was promised by God that through his descendants, God would establish a great nation and all the people and families of the earth shall be blessed through him. God was ultimately referring to our Savior, Jesus Christ but also that He (Messiah) would come through the Jewish people which is the nation of Israel. There is a trail in the genealogy of the Seed promised in Genesis 3:16 from Eve to Abraham and Sarah, to King David and Bathsheba, to Mary and Joseph, and ultimately to Jesus Christ as our King and High Priest.

From that viewpoint we see in the genealogy that Abraham's son Isaac, begat Jacob whose name was changed to Israel. It was Abraham's grandson, Jacob (Israel), and his twelve sons, and their children that made up the beginnings of this new nation of Israel.

During a severe drought in the land the children of Israel moved to Egypt. While they grew and prospered abundantly in Egypt, after 430 years they found themselves in bondage and slaves to the Egyptians.

Moses Brings the Law

We are all familiar with the next part of their history when Moses miraculously led the Jewish people out of Egypt. God continued to work many miracles among the Jewish people and provided guidance to them through Moses. Most everyone is also aware that God gave the law or the ten commandments to Moses, to give to the Jewish people. God not only gave Moses the law, but He also included guidelines for the Priesthood which included the sacrificial laws and systems. The law included the ten commandments and over 600 other ancillary laws that provided guidance to man to lead a holy life. It gave man a specific target to aim for and helped him identify when he missed the target. In other words, one of the purposes of the law was to provide us awareness of what sin is.

The law given to Moses included three categories of law: moral laws, civil laws, and ceremonial laws. These laws are comprehensive, covering a broad spectrum of life issues including, property rights, violence, dietary restrictions, slavery, workers compensation, treatment of animals, property damages and restitution, marriage laws, treatment of foreigners, economic laws, judicial laws, agricultural laws, health laws, laws of warfare, and religious laws including Holy Days and public holidays. If these laws are administered properly and followed appropriately in obedience, they can lead people to safely enjoy peaceful and loving lives in righteousness.

The problem is that everyone has a sin nature and even though they thought they could keep the law, and many times they wanted to keep the law, but they still found they continued to sin and break the law. Therefore, the law served another purpose, and they realized they were not able to meet the rigorous demands of the law. So, the law was good and served its purpose in that it gave them a clear target to aim for, and to avoid sin. But it also helped them realize they were not good enough to keep the law because they were sinners by nature. In other words, the law made them aware that they needed help to save themselves from their sins which was keeping them **separated from God or dead to God**.

This brings us back to Adam. Adam had only one law or restriction to follow – do not eat from the tree of knowledge of good and evil. When Adam ate of its fruit he rebelled against God, he was seeking **independence** from God. We know that Adam not only received the independence from God that he was seeking, but he passed that independence from God or separation from God on to every future generation of mankind through his seed. And now we can see how Adam's **independence** from God, has kept mankind from a continual relationship with God.

Sacrificial System

As mentioned, as part of the law, God provided guidance for the priesthood. Aaron, who was the brother of Moses, was chosen to be the high priest and Arron's sons were ordained to serve as priests under Aaron. They were all Levites, one of the twelve tribes of Israel, and God honored all the rest of the Levites as He chose them to serve Aaron and his sons in the priestly responsibilities. The priesthood had many responsibilities, which included handling all the sacrificial system and caring for the things of the tabernacle. There was a hierarchy with the high priest being the head and those under him were the priests, then the Levites who were not priests but were servants for the service of the sanctuary.

One of the many responsibilities of the priesthood was to administer the sacrificial system. As such, a primary purpose of the high priest was to intercede on behalf of the Israelites for their sins and reconcile them to God.

> *Hebrews 5:1-4 (NKJV) For every high priest taken from among men is appointed for men in things pertaining to God, that he may offer both gifts and sacrifices for sins. [2] He can have compassion on those who are ignorant and going astray, since he himself is also subject to weakness. [3] Because of this he is required as for the people, so also for himself, **to offer sacrifices for sins**. [4] And no man takes this honor to himself, but he who is called by God, just as Aaron was.*

This scripture clarifies one of the primary purposes of the high priest. He was to be a mediator that offers gifts and sacrifices for both men and for himself to God to atone for or cover for their sins. He is also a type or shadow of the true High Priest, Jesus Christ.

The sacrificial system itself was comprehensive and included guidance for the Israelites to offer sacrifices to God in a systematic manner that would be acceptable to God.

When we look at Genesis in chapter three, we see that God implemented the first blood sacrifice when He provided tunics of animal skin to cloth Adam and Eve. Then again in chapter four, we read about how Cain and Abel both offered sacrifices to God. It goes on to say, God respected Able and his offering, but He did not respect Cain and his offering.

While we don't specifically read that God previously had given Cain and Abel detailed guidance about how and what to give for an offering, it appears that God had previously instituted the sacrificial system that included the shedding of innocent blood of an animal when He provided tunics or animal skin as a covering for Adam and Eve to cover their shame. An innocent animal had to be sacrificed and its blood shed to remove the skin of that animal.

> *The purpose of the blood sacrifice is that the shedding of the innocent animal's blood caused its death and could become a substitute for man's death.*

This would have been the first blood sacrifice to cover the effect of man's sin. Most likely Adam and Eve understood that and communicated that to Cain and Abel. It is also possible that God spoke that directly to Cain and Abel because somehow Able knew it was appropriate to offer the firstborn of his flock and its fat. Then God conveyed His disappointment in Cain's sacrifice and spoke to Cain.

> *Genesis 4:7 (NKJV)* ⁷ *If you do well, will you not be accepted? And if you do not do well, sin lies at the door. And its desire is for you, but you should rule over it."*

Able followed God's guidance, and Cain did not. God offered a second chance to Cain and provided a clear warning and He even told Cain that he had authority over his thoughts. But instead of receiving God's offer, Cain became angry at God and killed his brother Able.

Now as we advance in time and we fast forward to Moses, God is providing detailed specific guidance in writing for the sacrificial system. God's instructions required the shedding of blood from certain animals to be offered as a sacrifice, to atone for, or cover man's sins. The sacrificial system was implemented to help man see that God provided a means of being reconciled to God through a **substitute**. Man's sins could be forgiven, and it also assisted in temporarily cleansing sin in his soul.

This sacrificial system is part of what is referred to as the Mosaic Law. God commanded these sacrifices and rituals. On the one hand, performance and practice of rituals and sacrifices was an act of obedience, trust, and repentance to bring forgiveness of sins through a **substitute**.

But God knew that no man would be able to fulfill the law. Even if man could be forgiven and temporarily meet the rigorous requirements of all the law, sin was still part of man's nature. Sin is part of our nature, and our flesh will always be vulnerable to sin until we physically die.

So, we see that one of the requirements of the high priest was to manage the priesthood and teach the law to the Israelites. As a man the high priest could easily identify with the human challenges of sin and the difficulties to always and completely be submissive to the law. Therefore, the high priest was to offer specific blood sacrifices to atone for man's sins.

We know from the scriptures that these animal sacrifices and shedding of their blood could only provide temporary relief of their sins. It could never bring complete salvation to mankind. While man's sins could be forgiven by shedding of blood through these innocent animal sacrifices, man would still go back and sin repeatedly because that is what his fleshly nature does. In other words, the blood of the animal sacrifice could not wash and remove man's sin nature. It could provide forgiveness for past sins, but because sin is in his fleshy nature he will continue to sin at some level. Even if a man died immediately after his sins were forgiven, he still has a sin nature, and his spirit is dead to God.

Therefore, a primary lesson we receive from these sacrifices is that a man's sins can be forgiven or atoned for by the shedding of innocent blood as a **substitute**. In other words, we know the wages of sin is death. All men have a sin nature and therefore all men must die and be separated from God for eternity. But God is showing man that there is a pathway to Godly forgiveness of sins through a substitution process and that process is by the shedding of innocent blood that causes the innocent animal to die as our substitute. The shedding of the blood of these innocent animals is accepted in God's eyes as an acceptable substitute to atone for or forgive man's sins.

Therefore, the first component of the purpose of the law was to bring an awareness to man that we have a sin nature, and we are all sinners and come short of the Glory of God. Because of Adam's sin we have all been born in the flesh with a sin nature. God never expected that we, on our own, could ever become holy enough to accomplish righteousness through the law. Since God cannot and will not dwell with sin, and we can't eliminate the nature of sin from our being, then there is nothing we can do on our own to save ourselves. We need something or someone greater than us to bring salvation to our lives.

> *A key point we learn from the law is that blood washes our sins through faith.*

The shedding of blood from these innocent animal sacrifices did not physically wash away sins. It was provided as a substitute for man to receive by faith the forgiveness of past sins.

Therefore, as we just learned, the second key purpose of both the law and sacrificial system was to be a tutor to teach us that God has prepared a means for us to obtain through faith the forgiveness of our sins through a substitute. The blood of an innocent animal represents our death as a substitute and will atone for or cover our sins and we can receive forgiveness of those sins through faith.

But this animal sacrifice will only provide forgiveness of our sins, it will not cleanse us of our sin nature. Therefore, it teaches us we still need a Savior to obtain true and complete salvation. This points us to the only complete means of salvation, which is faith in Christ. In other words, it helps us to identify that we can't save ourselves, and that God made allowance for a substitution, but we need to seek a Savior to help us restore our eternal relationship with God. The blood sacrifices offered up by the high priest provided for man's atonement, but it was only temporary. Both sin and the law point man to recognize that a Savoir is needed. Therefore, the law of sin and death, pointed man to Jesus Christ, who is our High Priest.

> Galatians 3:24-25 (NKJV) *Therefore the law was our tutor to bring us to Christ, that we might be justified by faith.* [25] *But after faith has come, we are no longer under a tutor.*

For thousands of years many people have been under the law of Moses. We have all tried at various times to be good enough and meet the conditions of the law. But we always fall backward and sin again.

One effect of the law outside of faith in Jesus Christ is that it brings condemnation and we become overwhelmed with guilt. So, we try harder to meet the requirements of the law. Then we sin again and find ourselves under condemnation and guilt again. Many people all over the world are still trapped in this cycle of sin, condemnation, and guilt. Without Christ there is no way to escape it. And we know that sin separates us from God.

There are also many born-again believers that possess victory over this condemnation but in ignorance of the complete value of salvation they can still fall short and still experience condemnation and guilt.

So, the Law taught us that man cannot save himself. The law was impossible to obey without a supernatural means of keeping it. So, the purpose of the law was to teach us and make us aware that we are sinners. The blood sacrifices of innocent animals taught us that by faith our sins could be forgiven but didn't wash away our sin nature. It also taught us that by faith a **substitution** was acceptable. This was a type and shadow of what was to come. It showed us a picture of the coming One who could save us, Jesus Christ. So, the ultimate purpose of the law was to point us to Jesus Christ as our Savior who is our **Substitute**.

In other words, the law and sacrifices teach two parts of the gospel message, that man is a sinner (law) and man needs a Savior (sacrifices). The completeness of the law and sacrificial system was given because the people told Moses they could keep God's commandments (Exodus 19:8). They thought they did not need faith or God's grace. They thought they were capable of pleasing God through their own ability to be good enough. However, they were continuing to establish their independence from God. God spoke to Moses only, and the mountain was covered with darkness, smoke, and wrath. The people did not want God to speak to them directly because they were afraid of Him, so they sent Moses to meet God and bring back the law.

> *They recognized God's superiority but also chose to believe*
> *they could manage sin on their own.*

Why were they afraid of God? It was because they were in sin, and they inherently knew God hated sin, so they stayed away from Him, while they worked on their sin with their own strength (**independent from God**)

How many people do you know that will tell you they are a good person and therefore they don't understand how God could let them go to hell for eternity because they won't pray the sinner's prayer and accept Jesus as their Lord? The law was given to help people like this to understand that they are not good enough to meet the righteous requirements of the law without the help of Jesus our Savior. If we are open and honest with ourselves, none of us have to look too far to see that we fall short of the mark and as hard as we may try, we can't obtain it on our own.

What is the Significance of the Blood?

God created all the creatures on earth including mankind with flesh and blood. Neither angels nor demons have flesh and blood. This unique feature of flesh and blood is only for earthly creatures. Sin entered this world when Adam allowed it into his flesh. Redemption therefore must come through man's flesh and blood. This redemption is not available to demons because they do not have flesh and blood.

In the natural world many scientists, medical researchers, and physicians have studied the blood of animals and of mankind. They have discovered that blood cycles through the body from a simple but complex pump with valves that we call the heart. As the heart pumps blood throughout the body through our vascular system, it regulates the volume and pressure of the blood flow. There are many defining properties and characteristics of blood and while this is not a biology book let us look at the basic physical purpose and function of blood in the natural.

As the blood is pumped out of the heart it carries oxygen, nutrients, and other cellular properties to all parts of the body which provide life to each of the components or members of our body. As the blood deposits these life producing elements into our bodies it also cleanses our body by collecting the impurities and damaging particles of things that are not good for us in our body. Then the impure blood cycles through a cleansing process through our liver and kidneys where those impurities are separated from the blood and discharged out of the body.

It then cycles back into the lungs to get replenished by getting fresh oxygen and other nutrients and then goes back through the heart to repeat the process over and over. If the heart stops pumping blood, there is no life circulating through the body and the body will cease to function, meaning the body dies. That is a general scientific overview of the blood.

Now let's look at what the Bible says about blood. Leviticus and Deuteronomy both refer to blood in depth about legal matters relating to the law. As such there are many references in these books regarding the blood of animals and of mankind.

> *Leviticus 17:11 (NKJV) [11] For the life of the flesh is in the blood, and I have given it to you upon the altar to make atonement for your souls; for it is the blood that makes atonement for the soul.'*

There are many scriptures such as this one that tell us life is in the blood and that includes both mankind and animals. There are many references in the Bible that tell us not to eat the blood of animals because there is life in the blood.

> *Leviticus 7:26 (NKJV) [26] Moreover you shall not eat any blood in any of your dwellings, whether of bird or beast.*

> *Genesis 9:4 (NKJV) [4] But you shall not eat flesh with its life, that is, its blood.*

> *Deuteronomy 12:23 (NKJV) [23] Only be sure that you do not eat the blood, for the blood is the life; you may not eat the life with the meat.*

These are just a few of the scriptures that tell us not to eat the blood. They don't say we can't eat the meat; they say don't eat the blood.

Leviticus 19:26 (NKJV) ²⁶ *'You shall not eat anything with
the blood, nor shall you practice divination or soothsaying.*

This scripture adds "*nor shall you practice divination or soothsaying.*" Divination and soothsaying refer to practicing fortune telling, witchcraft, magic, and sorcery. As we know God strictly forbids man from any involvement of such practices. Those who practice such things often incorporate satanic rituals wherein they drink blood. As such the Bible gives us many clear warnings not to practice these things, and not to drink the blood.

Hebrews 9:22 (NKJV) ²² *And according to the law almost
all things are purified with blood, and without shedding of
blood there is no remission.*

We see here in the New Testament that according to the law almost all things are purified with blood. Now we just reviewed that the blood in our body is cleansing our physical body. There are two distinct statements being made in this scripture. First "*according to the law*" which is referring to the old covenant, it says almost all things are purified or cleansed with blood. Then it says, without the shedding of blood there is no remission or in other words, no cleansing and forgiveness.

Leviticus 17:11 (NKJV) ¹¹ *For the life of the flesh is in the
blood, and I have given it to you upon the altar to make
atonement for your souls; for it is the blood that makes
atonement for the soul.'*

Now let's consider a corresponding Old Testament scripture. We see here in verse eleven that the shedding of blood is to make atonement for the soul. This implies that through faith in the promises from God the Israelites could have their minds and emotions cleansed from sin when following the sacrificial system of shedding an innocent animal's blood as God provided. While it could provide atonement for their souls it was still only the death of an innocent animal's blood sacrificed and therefore was unable to resurrect man's dead spirit. To meet the legal requirements to resurrect man's dead spirit would require an innocent man's blood as a sacrifice not that of an animal.

> *Leviticus 16:3 (NKJV)* ³ *"Thus Aaron shall come into the Holy Place: with the blood of a young bull as a sin offering, and of a ram as a burnt offering."*

> *Leviticus 14:25 (NKJV)* ²⁵ *Then he shall kill the lamb of the trespass offering, and the priest shall take some of the blood of the trespass offering and put it on the tip of the right ear of him who is to be cleansed, on the thumb of his right hand, and on the big toe of his right foot.*

> *Exodus 24:6-8 (NKJV) And Moses took half the blood and put it in basins, and half the blood he sprinkled on the altar.* ⁷ *Then he took the Book of the Covenant and read in the hearing of the people. And they said, "All that the LORD has said we will do, and be obedient."* ⁸ *And Moses took the blood, sprinkled it on the people, and said, "This is the blood of the covenant which the LORD has made with you according to all these words."*

> *Leviticus 16:15-16 (NKJV) "Then he shall kill the goat of the sin offering, which is for the people, bring its blood inside the veil, do with that blood as he did with the blood of the bull, and sprinkle it on the mercy seat and before the mercy seat.* ¹⁶ *So he shall make atonement for the Holy Place, because of the uncleanness of the children of Israel, and because of their transgressions, for all their sins; and so he shall do for the tabernacle of meeting which remains among them in the midst of their uncleanness"*

All these scriptures are samplings to establish that the blood of animals was used in the old covenant and when applied properly according to the requirements of the law the blood would provide for the atonement or forgiveness of man's sins.

> *It is also important to note the blood is not like a laundry detergent to wash away sins. It is **through faith** that God has provided forgiveness through the shedding of blood of the innocent animal.*

The shedding of the blood also signifies death. We know that when the blood stops circulating in the body there is no life circulating and imparting life into the elements of the body and therefore the sacrificial animal dies. In other words, the innocent sacrificial animal took on our sin, shed its blood and died. Then when the blood was properly applied according to the requirements of the law, the death of the innocent animal provided a **substitute** to atone for man's sins.

These old covenant blood sacrifices taught us about the important concept of faith and **substitution**. The wage of sin is death, so anyone who sinned had to die. However, God showed us in the old covenant that through faith a **substitute** could take our place in death, and that **substitute** would be considered acceptable. The substitute animal which would die, took man's place in death as the punishment for sin. This entire sacrificial system pointed to the animal as man's **substitute** but still required faith to receive the atonement.

Now let's step back for a moment and look at this process from a distance. The innocent animal's blood does not physically remove this sin from our being, nor does it physically cleanse our sin like a laundry detergent. It is by faith that man believed that this sacrificial ritual cleansed him from his sins. So, it required faith to recognize their sins were forgiven through this substitute.

However, these animal sacrifices were only temporary because they needed to be offered over and over again, year after year, for the sins of the people. That is because, while their sins were forgiven, they still had a sin nature. These substitute animal blood sacrifices provided atonement for their sins, but it did not remove their sin nature, and couldn't resurrect their dead spirit.

The blood of these old covenant animal sacrifices provided **atonement** for people's sins.

Atonement is the Hebrew word: "kaphar" which means to cover. It involves cleansing and forgiveness, but the emphasis is to cover, not replace.

The scripture tells us that the blood sacrifice makes atonement for sins. In other words, a blood sacrifice was made which covered the sins they had committed. To atone for sin means to cover sin. This is what atonement does. It covers the sins committed but does not remove the sin nature.

The core value or lesson to be learned from this sacrificial system was that by faith man can receive grace or the gift of forgiveness of our sins. The Jewish people embraced this concept. But the innocent animal's blood was not sufficient to resurrect our dead spirit and keep them from the ultimate destruction of sin. That would require the blood of an innocent man's blood. Therefore, it pointed them to have faith in the Son of man, the true coming Savior – Jesus Christ.

Gentiles and the Law

Now it is important to note that the law and sacrifices were given to the Jews. It was God's plan that they would ultimately share the good news of the Messiah, Jesus Christ which would include awareness of their knowledge of the law with the Gentiles. We know from history that they had some success bringing God's plans for redemption to the Gentile nations, but their success was limited.

But God did not leave the Gentiles without hope. The Apostle Paul tells us in Romans 1:18-32 that God has revealed Himself since the beginning of creation, with His invisible attributes being clearly seen and understood by the things that are made so they are without excuse. He goes on to say they knew of God but didn't glorify Him, they were not thankful but became futile in their thoughts and their foolish hearts were darkened. While professing to be wise they were exposed as fools and in their minds, they changed the glory of the incorruptible God into corruptible man made images of men and women and birds or four-footed animals, and other creeping things. And then Paul goes on revealing the effects of their choices.

> *Romans 2:14-16 (NKJV) for when Gentiles, who do not have the law, by nature do the things in the law, these, although not having the law, are a law to themselves, 15 who show the work of the law written in their hearts, their conscience also bearing witness, and between themselves their thoughts accusing or else excusing them) 16 in the day when God will judge the secrets of men by Jesus Christ, according to my gospel.*

Paul is reiterating in verse 14 that even the Gentiles have the law by nature. It is written in their hearts. We can all attest to the fact that even before we were born-again, we still could sense deep in our heart the difference between right and wrong. That is in our nature because God designed us to be that way. And then Paul confirms that our conscience bears witness to the law that God built into our nature. These are not all of the over 600 specific Jewish laws written in man's heart. Rather it is more of a general guide that God put into our nature.

Even still, the law doesn't keep mankind from sinning, but it makes us aware that we sinned. It shows us that we need a Savior.

Purpose of the Law

God had several purposes for giving the law to man. In addition to the points that have already been established and to add clarification, below is a list of a few of the purposes of the law.

The law sets out a Divine standard of righteousness. Psalms 19:7-10 and Romans 7:12-14.

To give a clear external definition of sin because of the inadequacy of man's conscience. Romans 3:20 and 7:7

To expose to all men their guilt before God. Romans 3:19

To illustrate the two major ways of God's dealing with man, which are seen in perfect balance of His own being: Law and Grace. John 1:17

To provide in the ceremonial law a temporary atonement for sin by which Israel could approach God in worship and upon the basis of which He could dwell in their midst. Hebrews 9-10

To show all the world that none can be justified (made righteous) by the law, but only through His grace through faith. Romans 3:19-22, 9:30-32, Galatians 3:10-16

Nature of the Law

Before closing this section let's consider the nature of the law. We just reviewed its primary purpose is to direct us to Jesus Christ.

> *Romans 7:12 (NKJV)* [12] *Therefore the law is holy, and the commandment holy and just and good.*

This scripture gives us some clarity. The law came from God and as such it is holy, just, and good. Despite the effect that sin has in man, the law is not to blame for man's guilt and condemnation. We have learned that sin brings shame and condemnation. The law makes us aware of our sins. Therefore, we should be grateful for the law.

> *Psalms 19:7-10 (NKJV) ⁷ The law of the LORD is perfect,*
> *converting the soul;*
> *The testimony of the LORD is sure, making wise the simple;*
> *⁸ The statutes of the LORD are right, rejoicing the heart;*
> *The commandment of the LORD is pure, enlightening the eyes;*
> *⁹ The fear of the LORD is clean, enduring forever;*
> *The judgments of the LORD are true and righteous altogether.*
> *¹⁰ More to be desired are they than gold,*
> *Yea, than much fine gold;*
> *Sweeter also than honey and the honeycomb.*

We see in this scripture that King David was grateful for the law. He understood the law was a gift from God. As such he directed and managed his thoughts accordingly. On the other hand, many people view the law as a burden that brings guilt and condemnation and keeps them from what they perceive as "having a good time" and to do the things that fulfill the desires of the flesh. King David's attitude was just the opposite because he understood the truth and was thankful to God for giving us His truth.

> *Psalms 19:13-14 (NKJV) ¹³ Keep back Your servant also from*
> *presumptuous sins;*
> *Let them not have dominion over me.*
> *Then I shall be blameless,*
> *And I shall be innocent of great transgression.*
> *¹⁴ Let the words of my mouth and the meditation of my heart*

Be acceptable in Your sight,
O LORD, my strength and my Redeemer.

Now we see that King David then goes on to ask the Lord for help to keep him from sinning. He recognized he was a sinner and that he needed help. In other words, he shows us how he was **dependent** on God throughout his life, and he recognized the value that the law brings.

> *Psalms 1:1-3 (NKJV)* [1] *Blessed is the man*
> *Who walks not in the counsel of the ungodly,*
> *Nor stands in the path of sinners,*
> *Nor sits in the seat of the scornful;*
> [2] ***But his delight is in the law of the LORD,***
> *And in His law he meditates day and night.*[3] *He shall be*
> *like a tree*
> *Planted by the rivers of water,*
> *That brings forth its fruit in its season,*
> *Whose leaf also shall not wither;*
> *And whatever he does shall prosper.*

And now we see that blessed is the man that delights in the law of the Lord and in the law, he meditates day and night. This is a substantial key to a successful life. It's all about the way we think. David proposed to follow and depend on God and did not want to do anything independent of God.

Let's look at another perspective regarding the law.

> *Romans 4:15 (NKJV)* [15] *because the law brings about*
> *wrath; for where there is no law there is no transgression.*

This scripture says the law brings forth wrath. Then how can we rejoice in the law if it brings wrath? For where there is no law there is no transgression. On the surface it appears that if the law was not brought forth, we would not have transgression. But if you recall transgression is sin but it relates to one having knowledge of sin and still crossing the line over to sin. More like a direct rebellion. In other words, a person can still sin even if they don't have knowledge of the law that defines sin.

Perhaps this allows us to follow what David said and we can still rejoice in God's laws. He shows us His pathways.

How does the law affect spirit, soul, and body?

One of the results of the law is self-awareness. We became aware of sin and its effects. As we become aware we begin to reason within ourselves. We can process the law and sin in our minds and our emotions and then determine how we manage it. Think, feel, and choose. If we follow David's lead we can rejoice in the law, and it will lead us to Jesus Christ who fulfilled the law for us, and He allowed us to be free from the law. Or we can choose to be under the law trying to fulfill every part of the law. The Apostle Paul described this as self-righteousness, because Jesus Christ was the only man that was able to fulfill the law.

Our body doesn't really know and understand the law. It only knows what the soul conveys to it. But the body does experience feelings, hunger, pain, cold/hot, and sexual desires. Our soul then can process all of the information from the body and use the law in part of the filtering process as it reasons within itself what to do.

If we are born-again, our spirit can receive guidance directly from the Holy Spirit. This ultimately gives us full freedom as we walk in the spirit. That is not a license to ignore the law. To the contrary.

> Galatians 5:22-23 (NKJV) But the fruit of the Spirit is love, joy, peace, longsuffering, kindness, goodness, faithfulness, [23] gentleness, self-control. Against such there is no law.

This is a guide to walking in the spirit. And we see that when we do there is no law against it!

CHAPTER 7

Perspective on Death

Death Is a Result of Sin

Romans 6:23 (NKJV) ²³ For the wages of sin is death, but the gift of God is eternal life in Christ Jesus our Lord.

Death entered the world through Adam's sin. If Adam had not sinned, death would not have had access to enter the world. We have seen that Adam's spirit died after he chose his independence from God and gave up his communion with God. This spiritual death is separating man from God. Through sin, death came, and so it continues to come ever since then. Death always comes through sin.

Romans 5:12 (NKJV) ¹² Therefore, just as through one man sin entered the world, and death through sin, and thus death spread to all men, because all sinned—

We learn three things from this verse.

1. Sin entered the world through one man – the first Adam.
2. Death came into the world through sin.
3. Death spread to all men because of sin.

Sin has permeated the spirit, soul, and body of all men. That is why it is vital that man receive God's life, because true and complete salvation will never be available in any type of human effort. Man alone is not capable of recovering from death. Sin must be judged before a man can enter God's Kingdom. Without the help of Jesus, at judgement time man will always be declared guilty of sin and therefore committed to eternal death because his very nature is sin, regardless of how good a person is on this earth. Even if it was what we might consider one tiny little sin, which is enough to declare us guilty and sentenced to eternal judgement in the confines of hell for eternity. That is all that death needs to have dominion over you. This is exactly why Jesus offered His life and died on the cross for us.

> *Throughout the Bible we see that the man who sins must die because of his sins.*

It is man's fleshly nature that sins, and therefore the man who sins must die. Only humanity can make amends for humanity. But herein there is a significant problem. Sin is part of man's nature or his humanity, so man's own death cannot provide compensation for his sin. We learned that our sins could be forgiven under the Old Covenant but that was not able to remove our sinful nature, nor could it resurrect our dead to God spirit.

Therefore, Jesus Christ came and took human nature upon Himself that He might be judged as a man. Jesus was not corrupted by sin. Remember the sinful nature of Adam was passed down to all men through his seed. But Mary the mother of Jesus did not know a man, (sexual relations) rather she was impregnated by God and gave birth to Jesus through her womb. The result was that when Jesus was born as man on earth, He was also born of God. His spirit, soul, and body were without sin. During His life on earth, He was able to fellowship with the Father and the Holy Spirit because His whole being was pure, without sin. His spirit, soul, and body did not have sin in them, but they were the same in form and function as our spirit, soul, and body. In other words, he was also subject to temptation just like we are. If Jesus could maintain the relationship with His Father and the Holy Spirit by staying free from sin and offering up His spirit, soul, and body as a sacrifice for us, and take on all the sins of the world for us, and rise from death, then He would be a perfect **substitute** sacrifice for us. So then if Jesus would be judged at death, no sin would be found in Him and therefore death could not hold Him because it had no legal right to claim Him, and He would be declared "not guilty." He would be a perfect sacrifice.

> *Romans 5:12 (NKJV)* [12] *Therefore, just as through one man sin entered the world, and death through sin, and thus death spread to all men, because all sinned—*

So again, we learn in Romans 5:12 that as Adam's sin was judged and His judgement passed through to all his descendants, we are born with the same sin nature. Now let's look at the difference between the effect of Adam and the effect that Jesus brought to us.

> *1 Corinthians 15:21-22 (NKJV) For since by man came death, by Man also came the resurrection of the dead.* [22] *For as in Adam all die, even so in Christ all shall be made alive.*

> *Romans 5:18-19 (NKJV) Therefore, as through one man's offense judgment came to all men, resulting in condemnation, even so through one Man's righteous act the free gift came to all men, resulting in justification of life.* [19] *For as by one man's disobedience many were made sinners, so also by one Man's obedience many will be made righteous.*

Now in a similar manner as the first Adam (representative of mankind), Jesus was judged but He was seen as righteous, His judgement is also passed on, and is made available to all mankind, that as man acknowledges he is a sinner and believes in Jesus' death, burial, and resurrection, Jesus would take on man's judgement!

> *Since all humans must be judged for their sin, and Jesus was in human form, and He was the first individual born of man that died and was sinless, He was judged and declared not guilty!*

Jesus Christ suffered in His spirit, soul, and body on the cross for the sins of the world. Jesus offered up His life to be judged. The good news of the Gospel is that Jesus was found to be innocent, declared not guilty, no sin was found in Him. So, Jesus Christ the last Adam (representative of mankind) because of His obedience, all men can be declared righteous if we trust and believe in His death, burial, and resurrection as our Substitute.

Legality of Death

Another perspective is that because Adam allowed sin to enter this world and through Adam's body his whole being – spirit, soul, and body became infected with sin and the very nature of Adam incorporated sin as part of his nature. As part of his nature or DNA, sin was passed on to every human being, and therefore every human also has a sin nature and has sinned, therefore death has a legal authority or jurisdiction to claim every living being on earth. We could say that Satan ushered sin into this world through deception, but remember, Adam had the legal authority to stop Satan. However, Adam rebelled against God by seeking his **independence from God**, which was the invitation for sin to enter into Adam and the world.

> *Romans 5:12 (NKJV) ¹² Therefore, just as through one man sin entered the world, and death through sin, and thus death spread to all men, because all sinned—*

This scripture is a written document showing that sin is what gave death the license and the legal right and jurisdiction to its claim in this world.

> *1 Corinthians 15:26 (NKJV)* [26] *The last enemy that will be destroyed is death.*

> *That is why Jesus came to earth as a man - to reconcile what Adam gave up and enforce the legal requirements that now operate over death.*

Let's make no mistake, as shown in this scripture – death is our enemy. It is easy to overlook that aspect of this scripture. While sometimes it may seem like death is a natural event because we have acknowledged it and it seems to be part of our natural environment, but remember it's not natural, death is our enemy. It was not God's desire for us to die. So, we should recognize that death is an un-natural enemy. God's desire was that mankind lives with Him in harmony for eternity.

> *John 10:18 (NKJV)* [18] *No one takes it from Me, but I lay it down of Myself. I have power to lay it down, and I have power to take it again. This command I have received from My Father."*

Jesus is speaking of His life as a man. Why did Jesus say nobody can take His life? What was different about Him as a man? He is not saying that He has more power than anyone wanting to kill Him (albeit Jesus Christ is more powerful). This scripture refers to a legal issue, not a discussion regarding Godly power. God is a just God, meaning that He established the law, and He will follow the law and fulfill the law. Jesus is saying that He is immortal, and that death has no legal authority over Him because there was no sin in Him. As a result, only Jesus had the authority to offer His life for us. No other man ever born has been sinless and therefore no other man could provide for man's salvation.

Remember, Mary the mother of Jesus did not know a man, she was a virgin. And we know that sin nature is passed down to the generations through man's seed. It was the Holy Spirit that fertilized Mary's Seed so that Jesus would be born without sin or sin nature. Just like Adam, Jesus was subjected to temptation, but Jesus did not surrender to the temptation of sin and therefore He did not know sin, and death never had a legal right or claim to Jesus. There were several times in Jesus's life that death tried to take Him, like when He was a baby and Herod killed all the babies in Bethlehem. Or in His ministry and the Pharisees tried to kill Him, or in the stormy seas when His disciples were convinced, they were all going to die in the storm. But death couldn't take Him because there was no legal right.

The Devil Came Illegally

> John 10:1-2 (NKJV) ¹ "Most assuredly, I say to you, he who does not enter the sheepfold by the door, but climbs up some other way, the same is a thief and a robber. ² But he who enters by the door is the shepherd of the sheep."

This is Jesus speaking and giving this illustration. He is saying that Satan entered the sheepfold illegally. A sheepfold is a pen or shelter for sheep. In this illustration sheepfold is referring to the world. The world was made for God's sheep, which is referring to us - mankind, and the sheepfold is our home, the world. Jesus is saying that anyone coming into the sheepfold (the world) without going through the door is a thief and robber because he is entering illegally. Jesus also says that He who does enter by the door legally is the Shepherd. Think about it – how did we get here into this world? Or we could ask, what is the legal method in God's design to enter this world?

We were all **born** into this world. The door is the womb of a woman. Jesus is the true Shepherd of the sheep and He entered legally. That is,

He humbled Himself to be born in the flesh as a man into this physical world. This and the fact that He was without sin provided for everything He needed to be the perfect human sacrifice for all mankind. Jesus was and is the sacrificial Lamb.

On the other hand, Satan came sneaking into this world as a snake to steal some of the authority that God gave to Adam (mankind). Satan was not born of a woman, he wasn't invited into this world, but came as a thief. He illegally snuck into this world to steal authority from Adam, kill him and destroy God's creation. It was the first crime of breaking and entering, grand theft, and murder. This world was made for man, not Satan.

To summarize this, all mankind and the animals are born of flesh and blood. That is how God designed and created this world to function. Satan and his demons are spirit (not flesh and blood) and came into this world illegally. God designed the world to be populated with creatures of flesh and blood. All flesh and blood come into this world through the womb. That is why Adam had authority to kick him out. Instead, Adam not only allowed Satan access, but he allowed Satan to usurp much of his God given authority over the earth.

It is very important that we recognize that Jesus offered Himself as a sacrifice, nobody took His life. And death could not hold Him.

> *Acts 2:24 (NKJV) ²⁴ whom God raised up, having loosed the pains of death, because it was not possible that He should be held by it.*

This scripture is referring to the resurrection of Jesus. Again, this is not a reference to the power of God, this is a reference to the legal authority of Jesus Christ. It is simply confirming that death could not keep hold of Him. Death did not have the legal jurisdiction or authority to hold Him, in fact, He took our sins on Himself as our **Substitute**, but death didn't have the right or authority to keep Him because our sins were judged at the cross and He was sinless.

Satan on the other hand came into the world illegally. Satan was not born into this world. God created the world to operate and function according to His design. And God's design required birth through a woman's womb for entrance into the world. Adam was given authority over the world, and Adam could have prohibited Satan from even being in the garden, but he allowed Satan to have access into the garden of Edan and Satan usurped Adam's authority and came into this world by deceiving Adam and Eve as a murderer, thief, and robber. When Adam and Eve sinned by eating the forbidden fruit, they allowed sin to enter the world. Their sin provided an opening and Satan entered, he brought death and the fallen angels in with him.

It is important to recognize that Jesus's goal was to die on the cross as our Substitute. As such He went through all the temptations of a man, physical pain, feelings of rejection and all kinds of emotional stress, and all kinds of torment and still He never sinned. He was identifying as a man in His death so that we can identify with Him in His resurrection. Since no sin was found in Him, death could not hold Him.

> *Jesus now had the legal authority over death, which provided legal authority for His resurrection.*

While every person was to be sentenced to eternal death, now those who accept Jesus in faith, through grace can share the victory of Jesus over death and we too can live for eternity with Him.

Adam's Death

Let's review some of the details of Adam's death once again.

*Genesis 2:17 (NKJV) [17] but of the tree of the knowledge of good and evil you shall not eat, for **in the day** that you eat of it you shall surely die."*

This scripture says, *"in the day,"* meaning this is a quick judgement and execution. As we have discussed his body lived for 930 years and his soul is immortal just like his spirit. But Adam's spirit died immediately when he sinned, however Adam's spirit was and still is immortal. His spirit did not cease to exist because it stayed in his body, but his spirit gave up his relationship with God, and God was his life source. The result was that Adam gained his **independence** from God. Therefore, his spirit is considered dead, or dead to God because there is no relationship. Without the salvation of Jesus Christ, death continues to have access to possess every person's spirit, soul, and body and it has the legal authority to claim every person born on earth because of Adam's sin.

As a result, every person who is born into this world after Adam's sin, was born with a dead spirit. And every person is born in the flesh with a sin nature. There is absolutely nothing that mankind could do of his own accord to re-establish his eternal life source with God. There was no work that he could do, he could not cease from sin, because he possessed a sin nature. He could not regenerate his spirit and bring it back to life with God. Man's spirit is dead, and Adam can't do anything on his own to fix it. In other words, sin destroyed his spiritual instinct to receive from God.

> *Adam and Eve's **spiritual transition** from life to death was a one-time situation because they were the only humans to experience it.*

A person can be religious, moral, educated, capable, strong, wise, pray regularly, or reason with God, but if he is not regenerated or born-again, he is still dead to God and without eternal spiritual instinct to receive from God.

Remember sin became a part of Adam's genes, he still has a spirit, but it is dead to God and every one of his descendants will be born spiritually dead to God. So, Adam experienced spiritual death and every one of Adam's descendants is simply born that way (dead to God). None of Adam's descendants including us, were born in the flesh with a spirit that was alive to God.

We also know that our body is just like Adam and Eve's body. Because of sin our body will die just like theirs, and just like theirs, our body will return to dust.

Two Deaths

The Bible tells us that just as there is a first and second birth there is also a corresponding, first and second death. The first death is the **physical consequence** of sin, and the second death is the **spiritual consequence** of sin.

First Death

The first death is a death that all people will experience, except for the born-again believers that are still alive on earth at the time of the rapture. The first death is the physical consequence of sin. As we know sin brings death. The first death is the experience of our physical body transitioning from life to death. Remember at creation our spirit and soul were breathed into Adam and he became a living soul. His body was just that, a physical body of flesh. His body had all its organs like the brain, heart, lungs and so on but there was no life source in his body until he received the Breath of Life, which brought life and animation to his body. In the same way when man's spirit and soul depart from his body the life source to his body is gone and his body dies and will decompose and returns to dust.

God's original plan for Adam and his descendants was that he would live for eternity in his physical body. But when Adam sinned, his sin invited sickness, disease, and calamity with it and consequently his body began to decay. Death destroys the physical body as the spirit and soul depart from the body.

As we reviewed in Genesis 3:19,20 man's body returns to dust. But this is only the physical realm that his body returns to dust. This is true for everyone that was born in the flesh. Everyone's body will return to dust except for the born-again believers that are still here on earth at the time of the rapture.

> *1 Thessalonians 4:17 (NKJV)* ¹⁷ *Then we who are alive and remain shall be caught up together with them in the clouds to meet the Lord in the air. And thus we shall always be with the Lord.*

This scripture is referring to the believers on earth when Jesus comes to take us up into the clouds to meet Him, in other words, the rapture. When we are caught up with Jesus in the clouds our body will be transformed from a mortal body into our new immortal body.

> *1 Corinthians 15:51-52 (NKJV) Behold, I tell you a mystery: We shall not all sleep, but we shall all be changed—* ⁵² *in a moment, in the twinkling of an eye, at the last trumpet. For the trumpet will sound, and the dead will be raised incorruptible, and we shall be changed.*

"We shall not all sleep" means that at the rapture our body will not die in the same manner that every other person experienced but *"we shall all be changed."* At this time, our physical body will be changed from corruptible to incorruptible and from mortal to immortal and our new body joined with our spirit and soul, will go up with Jesus and be with

Him for eternity. We will discuss our new "changed" body in more detail later in this book.

Keep in mind that the opportunity Jesus gave to us to be born-again will only be available until we experience the first death. While He is a God of second chances all the second chances are only available on this earth. Once our physical body dies, there **will not** be another second chance. Therefore, if you haven't yet made the decision to be born-again, it is extremely important to make it now, because you don't know when you will experience the physical or the first death.

Three Groups of People

This is a good time to introduce the concept that God has identified three groups of people in the world. All people born since and Eve will fit into one of these three groups. The groups are the Gentiles, the Israelites, and the Church.

The first group – The **Gentiles** are the nations (people) all around the world that are not Israelites or part of the Church. New Testament Gentiles means they do not believe in and accept Jesus Christ as the true Savior of the world because once they accept Jesus, they become part of the Church. There is no time restriction to be a Gentile, as there are New Testament and Old Testament Gentiles. In the Old Testament it was possible for Gentiles to believe in a coming Messiah just as it was possible for the Israelites to believe in the coming Messiah. Gentiles can generally be what we could refer to as good people, or they can be what we would refer to as evil people. They can even belong to a church, pray, and tithe, but they are not of Jewish descent, nor are they part of the Church, because they have not been born-again.

The second group - These are the **Jews** or **Israelites**. This is a group that has been chosen by God to be a special people. Their roots go all the way back to Abraham and continue through his descendants from his son Isaac and Jacob's twelve sons. God blessed them and they became a great nation and a world power. Unfortunately, they turned away from God and ceased to be a nation for well over two thousand years. As promised, God brought them back to their land to reunite as a nation and since 1948 they have been supernaturally continuing to prosper and grow as a nation. As a nation at the end of this age, they will be judged and will come to accept Jesus Christ as their Messiah.

The third group - This is the **Church**. The Church is composed of all the people from Group one or two, that have acknowledged themselves as sinners, and have recognized and believed in faith that Jesus died, was buried, and resurrected from the dead as Substitute for our sins. The Church is recognized as the bride of Christ. It includes only those believers from the time of Jesus to the time of the rapture. The identity of these three groups will help in the next section.

Where Does Our Spirit and Soul Go After Death?

Now that we have settled the eternal destination of our physical body (returns to dust), what about the destination of our spirit and soul?

There are two locations that are mentioned in the Bible that most people are familiar with. But that doesn't mean everyone believes it or acknowledges it. That said, a person's belief will not change the existence of these two eternal destinations, their belief will only effect where that individual's destination will be.

> *As we will continue to see, everyone has an opportunity to decide which location they want to be in for eternity.*

The most popular eternal destination is heaven, where God dwells. Because of His presence it is absolute beauty, filled with peace, joy, righteousness, which is the Kingdom of God. It is filled with life. While heaven is by far the best choice, and the most popular, and most desirable choice, many people will not choose this destination. The Bible is vividly clear that the Way is through Jesus Christ. Jesus Christ said, the Way is easy but the road to get there is narrow.

Then, for the second choice there is Hell or the Lake of Fire. It is the place of eternal judgement and punishment, for those whose names are not written in the book of life, and it is where Satan is sentenced to dwell for eternity. This is Satan's kingdom. All his demonic powers, rulers of the darkness of this age, spiritual hosts of wickedness including Death and Hades and all those people that never accepted and believed in Jesus will dwell in Hell for eternity.

While most people are aware of these two locations many are not familiar with the distinction of Hades, or they confuse Hell and Hades. Hades is like a waiting room for the spirit and soul of everyone in the Old Testament that physically dies. Additionally, those people in the New Testament that die but they were never born again. In other words, those that never accepted Jesus as Savior. This story of the rich man and Lazarus provides great insight to the environment in Hades.

> *Luke 16:19-31 (NKJV) "There was a certain rich man who was clothed in purple and fine linen and fared sumptuously every day."* [20] *But there was a certain beggar named Lazarus, full of sores, who was laid at his gate,* [21] *desiring to be fed with the crumbs which fell from the rich man's table. Moreover the dogs came and licked his sores.* [22] *So it was that the beggar died, and was carried by the angels to Abraham's bosom. The rich man also died and was buried.* [23] *And being in torments in Hades, he lifted up his eyes and saw Abraham afar off, and Lazarus in his bosom.* [24] *"Then he cried and said, 'Father Abraham, have mercy*

on me, and send Lazarus that he may dip the tip of his finger in water and cool my tongue; for I am tormented in this flame.'" 25 But Abraham said, 'Son, remember that in your lifetime you received your good things, and likewise Lazarus evil things; but now he is comforted and you are tormented. 26 And besides all this, between us and you there is a great gulf fixed, so that those who want to pass from here to you cannot, nor can those from there pass to us.' 27 "Then he said, 'I beg you therefore, father, that you would send him to my father's house," 28 for I have five brothers, that he may testify to them, lest they also come to this place of torment.' 29 Abraham said to him, 'They have Moses and the prophets; let them hear them.' 30 And he said, 'No, father Abraham; but if one goes to them from the dead, they will repent.' 31 But he said to him, 'If they do not hear Moses and the prophets, neither will they be persuaded though one rises from the dead.' "

From this scripture we can see a clear separation in Hades. A good side and a bad side. The decision regarding which side you are on is decided on earth before a person dies. At first glance it could seem like the rich go on one side and the poor go on the other. But that is not the issue Jesus is talking about. This has nothing to do with personal wealth. In verse 30 the rich man says to Abraham if you tell them they will repent. He is referring to their life decisions and their attitude, belief, and commitment and love toward God. There are many Old Testament saints on the good side in the Hades waiting room (Abraham's bosom).

Psalms 49:15 (NKJV) 15 But God will redeem my soul from the power of the grave, For He shall receive me. Selah

King David wrote this Psalm. He is one of those Old Testament saints that is now in the waiting room in Hades. But he is on the good side (Abraham's bosom). Their faith remains in God to be redeemed or delivered into God's presence for eternity.

Conversely, there are many individuals from the New and Old Testament time period waiting in torment on the bad side of Hades.

Now at some point everyone will be resurrected from Hades. But we need to look closer at this resurrection.

To further clarify the answer, where does our spirit and soul go, we need to continue identifying people by categories. The first category is whether you are a believer or non- believer.

1. **Non-believer**: At the first death (physical body) the spirit and soul of a non-believer will go to the bad side Hades which is essentially a waiting room until final judgement day. This includes all people that are non-believers regardless of when they were born. They will be resurrected for the final judgement. This resurrection is referred to as the second death.

2. **Believer**: For the spirit and soul of a believer we need to consider if this person was under the old covenant or the new covenant. Were they a believer before the resurrection of Jesus or afterwards? For simplicity we can refer to the believers from the period before the death and resurrection of Jesus as the Old Testament saints and those after the death and resurrection of Jesus as the New Testament saints.

   a. **Old Testament saints**: When an Old Testament saint died his body returned to dust and his spirit and soul went to the good side Hades (Abraham's bosom). This group of saints will have eternal life with God, but they are under the old covenant.

146

Their faith was and is in Jesus their coming Messiah, but they were not born-again because they were under the old covenant. In other words, they believed with anticipation that Jesus the Messiah would come to save them, but they physically died before Jesus provided for their salvation. This group will remain in Abraham's bosom and will be resurrected at the end of the tribulation and spend eternity with God.

b. **New Testament saints:** These are the believers that are born-again under the new covenant, this group is referred to as the "Church" or the bride of Christ. If their body died, or in other words they experienced the first death, then their body returned to dust and their spirit and soul went directly into the presence of the Lord.

i.   *2 Corinthians 5:8 (NKJV)* *8 We are confident, yes, well pleased rather to be absent from the body and to be present with the Lord.*

In this scripture Paul is saying that our spirit and soul goes directly into the presence of the Lord which is in heaven.

So, the first death includes believers and non-believers. We were all born in the flesh with a sin nature, and we have all sinned. It is easier for us to understand that non-believers will die because they didn't accept Jesus's gift of salvation and therefore their sins were not forgiven. However, if you're born-again you may ask why will I die in the flesh? Didn't Jesus die for **all** of my sins? The simple answer to both questions is yes, Jesus died for **all** our sins and if you're born again, He forgives you of **all** your sins. Your spirit is born-again and has become a new creature in Christ. But your flesh is still flesh and it still has a sin nature. Sin is still in your fleshly body and just like the unbeliever your sinful body will die and return to dust. This is the first death which is the physical consequence of sin. Therefore, ever since the resurrection of Jesus, after the first death of a believer, his spirit and soul will go to heaven and non-believers will still go to the torment side of Hades to await their final judgement.

Second Death

The second death is the spiritual consequence of sin. Remember we reviewed that death is a disconnection from the source of life. Where there is no life, there is death.

- Physically, we start with life, then we move toward death.
- Spiritually, we are born dead and in salvation we are resurrected to life.

When we are physically born, even though our bodies are animated, and we have full function of our faculties, in our spirit we are "dead in trespasses and sins."

> *Ephesians 2:1 (NKJV) ¹ And you He made alive, who were dead in trespasses and sins,*

This scripture refers to our spirit. We were born through our mother's womb spiritually dead but now those who are born-again are brought back to life in our spirit.

But those not born-again are different. Spiritual death or life is eternal. We were all born spiritually dead, we continue in our physical life on earth to be spiritually dead, and when we physically die (first death) our spiritual death carries on into eternity because our spirit and soul are immortal. Again, this is the spiritual consequence of sin. It is sin, which separates us from God, who is our life source. Therefore, if we still possess our sins in our spirit, we have no life because we are not connected to a life source, which could only be in God.

We learn from the book of Revelation that at the end of the millennial period there will be a great white throne of judgement. This judgement describes the second death.

> *Revelation 20:13-15 (NKJV) The sea gave up the dead who were in it, and Death and Hades delivered up the dead who were in them. And they were judged, each one according to his works. *[14]* Then Death and Hades were cast into the lake of fire. **This is the second death.** *[15]* And anyone not found written in the Book of Life was cast into the lake of fire.*

> *Revelation 21:8 (NKJV) *[8]* But the cowardly, unbelieving, abominable, murderers, sexually immoral, sorcerers, idol-aters, and all liars shall have their part in the lake which burns with fire and brimstone, **which is the second death.**"*

The second death is the great white throne judgement. This judgement is for those that rejected Jesus. It includes Satan and his demons, including Death and Hades. It also includes everyone born on earth whose names are not found in the Book of Life. Those that rejected Jesus while living in the world are those whose names are not found in the book of life. These will all be judged according to their works. Some might say, but I didn't reject Jesus, I just didn't follow Him or believe in Him. At this judgement everything will be revealed and nothing including every thought you had throughout your life on earth cannot be hidden. This judgement is final and there will not be any appeals. All of these will be sentenced to torment for eternity in the Lake of Fire. Many of these non-believers may think to themselves, "I have lived without Jesus in my life on earth and I am a good person. I give to the poor; I am nice to others, and I have enjoyed my life. I will be ok for eternity without God." This is a lie and deception from the devil. All of these people will live in hell with the devil and all his demons to be tormented for eternity.

Now is the time to make sure you accept Jesus and ensure that your name is written in the book of life. If you are a believer, you are born-again and you **will not** be part of this judgement (second death). Believers will only see the first death and they will all receive new, changed bodies.

But all the non-believers will be involved in both the first and second death. With this understanding of death, it helps to understand the significance of Adam's choice in the garden of Edan. Still today, for all of us on earth, we all have the opportunity to choose life or death.

A primary focus in the Bible is for every person born on earth to choose life or death. In other words, where he wants to spend eternity (his forever retirement home) and who he wants to spend that time with. The Bible is like a brochure that exposes the benefits or the realities of the truth behind the two choices we have.

When it is understood, choice #1 is by far the most popular and most desired. That is to live with God in His Kingdom which is righteousness, peace, and joy. The environment is far superior to a five-star hotel and travel arrangements are always first class.

Or we can pick choice #2. This is a default choice if we neglect to choose option #1 before our physical death. Many choose this option because they didn't read the brochure (Bible) and were deceived. As a result, this alternative is to spend eternity with Satan which is death (separation from God) and all of Satan's minions with evil and destruction and torment. Accommodations are very uncomfortable and filled with anxiety, fear, condemnation, guilt and all forms of evil.

From this perspective when we remove the blinders it is an easy decision to choose life. But we need to make that decision before we physically die and leave our physical body.

CHAPTER 8

Introducing the Last Adam

In the last three chapters we looked at sin, the law, and death. We discussed the definition of sin and how the law helped to make it clear that we are sinners, and as sinners we will die, therefore we need a Savior, someone in the form of a man. Someone that meets the legal qualifications to overcome and defeat the power of sin and death. Someone that has obtained legal authority to wash away our sins and resurrect our spirit from death. Without a true Savior all of mankind is destined to spend eternity in hell with Satan. We also know that God is holy which means that sin cannot be in His presence. In other words, we cannot enter the kingdom of God if we possess sin. So, the picture of this problem becomes vividly clear. Because of Adam's sin, every person is born with a sin nature and sin cannot exist in God's presence. We inherited our sin nature from Adam; therefore, sin is part of our nature, and it is our own sins that we need to be saved from.

Now with that summary in mind, we know from Genesis 3:15 that God had already introduced that there will be a way for man to be redeemed from the judgement of Adam's sin.

> *Genesis 3:15 (NKJV) ¹⁵ And I will put enmity*
> *Between you and the woman,*
> *And between **your seed and her Seed**;*

He shall bruise your head,
And you shall bruise His heel."

God is speaking here about the promise of Jesus Christ which is *"her Seed"* that will bruise Satan's head. Jesus Christ will come and redeem or purchase back that which Adam gave up and He will restore not only that but much more.

> *John 3:16 (NKJV) ¹⁶ For God so loved the world that He gave His only begotten Son, that whoever believes in Him should not perish but have everlasting life.*

This is a popular and well-known scripture and Jesus Christ is *"her Seed"* and our Savior that is referenced. God the Father sent Jesus Christ to bring salvation to mankind. Let's look deeper at what He did for us, how He did it, and what it means to us.

Identifying the Two Adam's

The first Adam and the Last Adam both represent mankind. In this case we are not referring to their names. As a representative for all of mankind the first Adam's sin affected all mankind, and sin became part of mankind's DNA. Since the first Adam was the representative of all mankind, we did not have a choice, the first Adam made it for us, and we were condemned to death.

On the other hand, also a representative of all mankind, the Last Adam's sinless death also affected all mankind, and His death and resurrection are made available to all mankind that believes on Him. Let's look at this in more detail.

> *1 Corinthians 15:45 (NKJV) ⁴⁵ And so it is written, "The first man Adam became a living being." **The last Adam** became a life-giving spirit.*

Let's start by identifying who the first and last Adam is. Why is this scripture talking about a first and last Adam? God named the first man that He created Adam, so it is simple to determine that he is the first man whom this scripture is referring to. The word Adam in Hebrew can refer to an individual's proper name, but it also refers to a general noun – "mankind". Therefore, if we are making a statement about **"all of mankind,"** as an alternative, we could say **"all of Adam."** While that can be considered a proper statement, it is not generally the way we would say it in the English language. In the Old Testament the word Adam is used over 500 times as a general noun. So, it is used far more often in scripture as a noun rather than referring to the individual name Adam.

This scripture refers to the first and the Last Adam as being representatives of all mankind. Perhaps we could use the term prototypes or models that the rest of mankind would or could become. Or we could simply say, after His kind.

When God created the first man Adam or mankind, He created him to reproduce according to his own kind, the image or likeness of his nature or DNA. The first man Adam was created without sin, but he chose to eat the forbidden fruit that incorporated sin into his being and his spirit died to God. In other words, sin became part of his being, or nature, or his genes. As such, that sin nature became a natural part of all mankind or all of Adam. This scripture is defining the natural part of the first man Adam or mankind and incorporating a focus towards his body and soul, because his spirit died to God.

On the other hand, the Last man Adam became a life-giving spirit. Now following that concept that through one man all those that follow will reproduce after His own kind, the Image or likeness of His Nature or DNA. We are now referring to Jesus who died for us, for our sins and those who believe and accept Him can share in His nature and DNA as well.

Now with that in mind let's consider the next scripture that further clarifies this point.

> *1 Corinthians 15:46-49 (NKJV) However, the spiritual is not first, but the natural, and afterward the spiritual. ⁴⁷ The first man was of the earth, made of dust; the second Man is the Lord from heaven. ⁴⁸ As was the man of dust, so also are those who are made of dust; and as is the heavenly Man, so also are those who are heavenly. ⁴⁹ And as we have borne the image of the man of dust, we shall also bear the image of the heavenly Man.*

Verse 47 says the first man was made of the earth, made of the dust and he goes on to say, "*As was the man of dust,* **so also are those who are made of dust**". This is simply a statement saying that we all inherited the first Adam's genes. In other words, we were reproduced after our own kind. There are certain aspects of his genes that are naturally still part of our beings today as each person is born in the flesh or naturally through our mother's womb and like him our body will also return to dust.

But the last Adam is the Lord from heaven. This is clearly Jesus Christ, the Messiah. Now back to verse forty-six clarifies the first Adam representative was the natural, from the earth, dust, and this is obvious that it is referring to his fleshly body and our body will follow the same path as his body by returning to the dust. The last Adam representative is spiritual from heaven. Likewise, those of us that believe on Him will come alive spiritually and our spirit will also follow Him to heaven where He came from.

> *Our natural body will follow the first Adam and return to dust. Our spirit will follow the Last Adam and return to heaven.*

1 Corinthians 15:45 (NKJV) [45] *And so it is written, "The first man Adam became a living being." The last Adam became a life-giving spirit.*

We have already learned about the first Adam representative and how God breathed into his flesh, and man Adam became a living being. The emphasis of living beings is on the soul or soulish realm and incorporating the physical body. Now we see the last Adam representative became a life-giving spirit. **This last Adam representative is Jesus Christ**. And the emphasis is focused on the spirit. It is vital to understand the role and the impact that each of these two men have in the life and death of all humanity. The first man representative became a living being and the last man representative became a life-giving spirit. What is the difference?

Romans 5:17 (NKJV) For if by the one man's offense death reigned through the one, much more those who receive abundance of grace and of the gift of righteousness will reign in life through the One, Jesus Christ.)

Let's put these scriptures together. The first Adam representative sinned and consequently he died. It says, *"death reigned"* is referring to his whole being and all of mankind. It began with his spirit that died immediately and ultimately included his soul and body (flesh). The issue is that his sin became part of his nature and was passed down to his descendants through his DNA, and sin brings forth death. In simple terms, every person ever born in the flesh is born with a spirit that is dead to God, and his flesh is alive to sin so his flesh will also die.

The follow up is the good news of the Gospel. Just as in the first Adam representative sin spread to all mankind and death reigned through him, now through one man's righteousness (last Adam representative, Jesus Christ), the benefits of His death and resurrection are available by grace for those who believe in Him and accept Him in faith.

Romans 5:15 (NKJV) [15] *But the free gift is not like an offense. For if by the one man's offense many died, much more the grace of God and the gift by the grace of the one Man, Jesus Christ, abounded to many.*

The offense in this verse is referring to the first Adam representatives' sin and because of his sin, many have died an eternal death. He had a choice, and he chose death on behalf of all of us.

The gift is the grace of God – the death, burial, and resurrection of Jesus Christ. He took our sins and died on the cross in our place. He was our **Substitute**. This gift is now available to everyone, and they can receive an abundance of grace, the free gift of eternal life in righteousness. He restored to all of us the same choice the first Adam made on behalf of all mankind, but now we have that choice again because of what Jesus did. God views the death of Jesus Christ as the death of all the people in the world who choose to follow Him. His holy humanity suffered death for everyone in the world and if they choose to believe in Him, they can have eternal life with Him.

So, now you have been introduced to the last Adam representative, our Savior, Jesus Christ. He is referred to as the last Adam because just like we received natural life from the first Adam representative, now Jesus Christ provides us spiritual life. Each of these men have a significant role in defining what and who Adam or mankind is, and ultimately both the natural and spiritual life is available to all the generations.

The Life of the Last Adam, Jesus Christ

Let's continue to add to our quick overview of Jesus including a few reference points in the Bible as to who Jesus Christ is and more specifically His role in the history of mankind. There are scriptures in every book of the Bible that speak of and point to Jesus Christ as the Savior of the world and mankind. In this chapter we will highlight a few of those references, some that are obvious and some that were written as a mystery. As we reveal some of these references, we will also be substantiating why Jesus was more than qualified for this job as the world's Savior.

We know He is introduced in the first sentence in the Bible. *"In the beginning God created the heavens and the earth."* The Hebrew word for God is Elohim, which incorporates the Trinity – Father, Son, and Holy Spirit. So, Jesus Christ is the Son of God. We already discussed that He is the Seed referenced in Genesis 3:15 that will give us victory over Satan and that allows us to obtain salvation.

We have also discussed and learned through the Mosaic law, that God allowed for a provision that an innocent animal such as a lamb could be slain so that its blood could atone for man's sins as a **substitute** for man's death. This atonement was only for his past sins not for future sin.

> *Romans 6:7 (NKJV)* [7] *For he who has died has been freed from sin.*

This is a key scripture. We know the penalty of sin is death. So, Jesus took on our sin and was crucified – He came to earth to die for us so that we could be able to identify with His death as our Substitute. As we believe on Him and identify with His death, then sin has no power over us.

This scripture tells us the way to be free from sin is to die. As we discussed, in the Old Testament an innocent animal can die as a **substitute** for our sin. This was part of the Mosaic law and as the high priest symbolically transferred the sins of the people to the innocent slain animal, then by faith, the Jewish people's sins were atoned or forgiven. They were essentially cleansed from those past sins, and their conscience was cleared. But again, it couldn't resurrect their dead spirit. However, this was a major point in man's history to recognize that a **substitute** was acceptable, and an innocent animal could die in place of man for man's sins to be atoned through faith in God's promise. The main weakness or problem was that this innocent animal could not resurrect their dead spirit. This was part of the requirements of the law of sin and death as seen in Romans 5:17. Through one man's sin all mankind is destined for death, but the reverse part is also true; "much *more those who receive abundance of grace and of the gift of righteousness will reign in life through the One, Jesus Christ*". This sacrificial system for an innocent animal was intended as an example or shadow of what was coming - Jesus Christ.

It all points to Jesus Christ as our **Substitute** who was able to meet all the requirements for our sins to be forgiven once and for all. And because He met all the legal requirements to cleanse our sins, He was also raised from the dead, and therefore we can not only unite with Him as our Substitute in His death, but also in His resurrection.

What Were Jesus' Qualifications?

So how did Jesus qualify as our **Substitute**? What were the requirements? As we already know there were many scriptures prophesying the coming of Jesus the Messiah.

Genealogy of Jesus – He Had to be a Man

We already discussed that Abraham was the father of the Jewish people – the nation of Israel. God promised Abraham that through his son Isaac and his descendants, the nation of Israel would be established. From Israel, God would bring forth the Messiah, and through Him all the nations of the world would be blessed eternally.

Several scriptures show the genealogy from Abraham to King David. We also know that God's word says that the Messiah would come through the line of David.

> *Let's look at the blood lines and the genealogy of Jesus and His parents, Mary and Joseph.*

There are many scriptures providing genealogy in the Bible, but we will focus on two specific scriptures for our purpose here. Specifically In Luke chapter 3:23 we see the genealogy of Jesus all the way back to Adam and Eve. We also see in Mathew chapter 1 the genealogy of Jesus that goes back to Abraham. We are going to highlight key differences in these two listings of genealogy and establish the relevance of the genealogy to support that Jesus is the true Messiah.

These two scriptures split the genealogy after David, into two different lines. Luke follows the lineage from David through his third son Nathan who was born in Jerusalem down to Mary the mother of Jesus. Mathew takes the lineage from David to his son Solomen down to Joseph the adoptive father of Jesus.

> *Matthew 1:1 (NKJV)* [1] *The book of the genealogy of Jesus Christ, the Son of David, the Son of Abraham:*

Before getting into the details of each father, Matthew 1:1 opens the genealogy of Jesus with an overview to highlight and to put the focus on these three men (Jesus, David, and Abraham. This is to confirm the prophecy that the Messiah would come through the descendants of Abraham and continue through David and to Joseph and ultimately to Jesus.

It is worth noting that the gospel of Mathew was written by a Jew to the Jews about a Jew. The gospel of Mathew is intended to establish Jesus as the Messiah, King of the Jews and confirm that Jesus is the legitimate heir to the throne of King David. As such the genealogy goes from David to Solomon and through all of the descendants of the kingly line of David all the way to Joseph the adoptive father of Jesus.

In Jeremiah 22 we read that Jeconiah was the last king in David's dynasty to sit on the throne as king of Israel. This was due to the fact that they turned away from God. Nonetheless, just as God promised we can still see the genealogy continue from king Jeconiah to Joseph, the adoptive father of Jesus. Therefore, if the Israelites would have remained faithful to God, the kingship would have continued through to Joseph. Now in those days adoption was common. In fact, Ceasar Agustus who was the most powerful leader of the world back then was an adopted child. Therefore, it was well recognized that an adopted son could legally be the heir to the throne of a kingdom. Perhaps God just wanted to assure the world that He considers adoption as an approved legitimate legal process.

> *Luke 2:4-5 (NKJV) Joseph also went up from Galilee, out of the city of Nazareth, into Judea, to the city of David, which is called Bethlehem, because **he was of the house and lineage of David,** [5] to be registered with Mary, his betrothed wife, who was with child.*

This scripture confirms that Joseph went through the legal process of adoption because he went to Bethlehem to register his family. The point is that if Israel remained in power with a King on the throne of Israel, we could follow the lineage from David to Solomen ... to Jeconiah to..... Joseph and finally it would have transferred to Jesus as the adopted son of Joseph. So, now we can see that Jesus had the legitimate right to the throne as the adopted son of Joseph. That also fulfills many prophecies that the Messiah would come through the kingly line of David. In summary the book of Mathew was written primarily with the Jews in mind and this lineage identified Jesus as the King of the Jews just as it was written on the cross – King of the Jews.

Now let's consider Luke 3:23 which begins with lineage with Joseph the husband of Mary all the way back to Adam. Now the book of Luke was written primarily with the Gentiles in mind. Luke the author of the book was a physician and much of his focus was to establish the focus that Jesus came to this world as a man.

Most biblical scholars agree that this is the genealogy of Mary, the mother of Jesus. Though it starts with being the son of Joseph, the son of Heli, it is believed this is a reference to Joseph as the son in law of Heli to stay in line with the Jewish custom of recognizing the man even though it was Mary's genealogy.

So, we can see that the Seed of Eve mentioned in Genesis 3:16 can be specifically traced from Adam and Eve to Abraham and Sarah, to David and Bathsheba, to Joseph and Mary, to Jesus Christ our Savior. The focus here is to recognize Jesus' connection to all of humanity all the way back to the first Adam. It also establishes the biological relationship from Mary as the mother of Jesus up through David to Abraham and to Adam and Eve.

We should mention again that Mary was impregnated by God. Remember the seed of sin was in all men and when a man's seed impregnated a woman the seed of sin was automatically transferred to the child. That is why Jesus was born without sin, because His real Father, God did not transfer the seed of sin. The effect was that Jesus was born as a man without sin, just like the first Adam began his life without sin. Nonetheless, Jesus was raised by the appointed parents just as God planned.

Beyond Jesus' blood line there are other requirements that were needed.

He had to be born on earth as a man. In other words, He had to come into this world the same way every other person does – through the womb of a woman, or in other words, through their mother. We know that Jesus was born through His mother, Mary. It is important to note that although He is a member of the Trinity, He left His position on the throne as God in heaven and humbled Himself to become a man.

Because of this requirement to be a man, Jesus most frequently referred to Himself as the Son of Man. He was also the Son of God and referred to Himself that way at times, but much more often He referred to Himself as the Son of Man.

> *Philippians 2:8 (NKJV) And being found in appearance as a man, **He humbled Himself and became obedient** to the point of death, even the death of the cross.*

Additionally, He had to be without sin. There are two critical points to recognize on this issue. Because of the first Adam's sin every person is born with sin in their nature. That sin is passed down through the genes of the father (not the mother) to every person born. That issue in and of itself disqualifies every person born of a woman.

But the Bible tells us that Mary did not know a man (physical, sexual relations). She was impregnated by God, who is without sin, but Jesus was still born of a woman. Therefore, Jesus was born as a natural person just like every other human being but He didn't have a sin nature and so He was born without sin.

Jesus Had to Experience Temptation and Still Be Sinless

Similarly, the first Adam was created without sin. So, both the first Adam and the last Adam started their lives on earth without sin in their being. We already know the first Adam representative later allowed sin to enter in. The last Adam was kind of like a do-over or a second chance.

So, now the next critical point about Jesus, as the last Adam is that He had to continue being without sin in His life so He could be a qualified **Substitute**. In other words, both Adams started out the same (without sin), but the last Adam had to finish without sin to qualify as our **Substitute**.

In the scripture we just read in Philippians 2:8 He humbled Himself, and He became obedient. This is a key point we can learn from Him. He became obedient after He humbled Himself. Humility is an important characteristic to be an effective leader.

The point to recognize is that while Jesus was born without sin, He still needs to live His life on earth without sin. But remember that He was born with a natural body and soul just like ours.

> *Luke 2:51-52 (NKJV) Then He went down with them and came to Nazareth, and was subject to them, but His mother kept all these things in her heart. ⁵² And **Jesus increased in wisdom and stature, and in favor** with God and men.*

This scripture is referring to Jesus when He was growing up as a boy. He had to grow in wisdom and stature in favor with God and man. It was not automatic. In other words, this scripture validates that He was just like us. He had to grow and develop physically, mentally, emotionally, and spiritually. He was subjected to sin just like any of us but perhaps even more so. God wanted to be clear that Jesus faced temptation and still overcame temptation and desires of His flesh.

Just like Adam and Eve were tempted of the devil with the fruit from the tree of knowledge of good and evil, so Jesus had to be tempted in a similar manner before He could confirm His rights to taking back dominion. Jesus fully established that He was a man and dealt with similar life issues as every other person. He purposed to identify with man's sinful nature but remain without sin.

> *Hebrews 5:1-2 (NKJV) For every high priest taken from among men is appointed for men in things pertaining to God, that he may offer both gifts and sacrifices for sins. ² He can have compassion on those who are ignorant and going astray, since he himself is also subject to weakness.*

This is describing the role of the high priest. As a man, the high priest is also subject to weakness and temptation. One of his primary roles was to offer blood sacrifices of innocent animals to God on behalf of the people to atone for their sins. Again, this is a type and shadow of things to come (Jesus Christ, the Messiah).

> *Hebrews 5:3-4 (NKJV) Because of this he is required as for the people, so also for himself, to offer sacrifices for sins. ⁴ And no man takes this honor to himself, but he who is called by God, just as Aaron was.*

We see here just how important this role of the high priest was. The role of the high priest was a specific calling, directly appointed by God. This was meant to be a type or shadow of things to come.

> *Hebrews 5:8-10 (NKJV) though He was a Son, yet **He learned obedience by the things which He suffered.** ⁹ And having been perfected, He became the author of eternal salvation to all who obey Him, ¹⁰ called by God as High Priest "according to the order of Melchizedek,"*

Now we can see this role of the Old Testament high priest was pointing to Jesus. *"Though He was a Son, yet He learned obedience by the things which He suffered."* There is so much to learn from this verse. This is the second scripture that again validates His humanity because He had to learn obedience. He didn't learn this in the classroom. He learned obedience from on-the-job training, real-time experience in His sufferings. This is a short rabbit trail but it's important to note that even Jesus learned obedience by the things He suffered. Obedience is something we learn through experience and humility.

Jesus' Temptation is Further Validated

To take it another step further, at the beginning of Jesus' ministry, the Holy Spirit led Him to the mountain to be tempted. Jesus didn't just happen to be in the wrong place and fell into temptation. He was led by the Holy Spirit to make sure everyone could see He overcame temptation. So, this was about 4,000 years after the devil tempted Adam and Eve he tried the same trick on Jesus, the Last Adam.

> *Matthew 4:1-11 (NIV) Then Jesus was led by the Spirit into the wilderness to be tempted by the devil. ² After fasting forty days and forty nights, he was hungry. ³ The tempter came to him and said, "If you are the Son of God, tell these stones to become bread." ⁴ Jesus answered, "It is written: 'Man shall not live on bread alone, but on every word that comes from the mouth of God.'" ⁵ Then the devil took him to the holy city and had him stand on the highest point of the temple. ⁶ "If you are the Son of God," he said, "throw yourself down. For it is written:"*
> *"He will command his angels concerning you, and they will lift you up in their hands, so that you will not strike your foot against a stone.'"*
> *⁷ Jesus answered him, "It is also written: 'Do not put the Lord your God to the test.'"*
> *⁸ Again, the devil took him to a very high mountain and showed him all the kingdoms of the world and their splendor. ⁹ "All this I will give you," he said, "if you will bow down and worship me."*
> *¹⁰ Jesus said to him, "Away from me, Satan! For it is written: 'Worship the Lord your God, and serve him only.'"*
> *¹¹ Then the devil left him, and angels came and attended him.*

The devil tried to deceive Jesus just like he did with Eve. Similarly, as with Adam and Eve, Satan did not have authority to command Jesus to do anything. Jesus had a free will, so all that Satan could do was to deceive Jesus and tempt him just like Adam and Eve. Satan perceived that Jesus was weak because He had been fasting 40 days. Now remember Jesus was on earth in the form of man. Imagine fasting for forty days, how would you feel? At a minimum He would have been hungry, tired, and physically weak. He had a fleshly body and soul just like us, except there was not a sin nature in Him. However, remember that at the time when Adam and Eve were tempted neither of them had sin nature either. The devil tried to question Jesus and get Him to open the door of temptation with,

- Lust of the flesh
- Lust of the eyes
- The pride of life.

Jesus would have no part of it and showed us how to overcome the devil and temptation using the sword of the Spirit – the Word of God. We are getting insight about God's character as He sets the example for how we should operate.

As we follow the life of Jesus in the scriptures, we can see that Jesus always maintained a selfless lifestyle. He knew and understood His purpose on earth. His purpose was to live a sinless life on earth, and then take on all the sins of the world throughout history to the cross and die as our Substitute.

In summary we can see that God planned the perfect process for mankind to return to God and have eternal life with Him. He sent His only Son. He had to come as a man, and we see the proof and the miracle of that process in this chapter. As a "Man" is a reference to mankind's whole being but with emphasis to his physical body and soul, which is the "natural man" or as we learned "flesh."

However, we can't lose sight of the fact that as a man Jesus also has a spirit. The most critical element of this chapter is to understand that as our Substitute, Jesus' spirit, soul, and body died for our sins, and because of His innocence, His spirit, soul, and body were also resurrected. If we believe on Him, we can identify with His death and resurrection and receive the benefits that only He could provide.

CHAPTER 9

---·❊·---

Salvation

Two Births

L et's first remember that Adam and Eve were created by God, not born of God and it's important to think through the difference between the two events. After God created Adam, He said this is very good! He did not create Adam with sin. Sin entered Adam because Adam made a bad decision in the garden and chose death. Every human being after Adam, was born of man, meaning every child inherits his father's nature or DNA. In other words, every person after Adam and Eve came into this world through the womb of their mother. Simply put we refer to this as birth. We have already reviewed a deeper understanding of death, and we reviewed that the Bible tells us there are two deaths and we need to accept and receive our salvation before our first death, while we are here on earth so that we can avoid the second death. Now let's take a closer look at birth. Jesus tells us that to receive eternal salvation we must be born-again, and that there are two births.

Born-Again

As we look at the process to be born again let's consider these three events that shape the history of mankind.

1. God created mankind. (This describes Adam and Eve)

2. Man was born of man. (This describes every human being conceived in a woman)

3. Man was born of God. (This describes every human being that is born-again)

When you read John 3:1-15 you will see that Jesus told Nicodemus he had to be born again. Nicodemus was a Pharisee and a ruler of the Jews. Nicodemus was likely an older man that had much knowledge of the Old Testament scripture and Jesus told him unless one is born again, he can't see the Kingdom of God. This was troubling to Nicodemus and as he reasoned in his mind, he asked Jesus, how can a man enter a second time into his mother's womb and be born again?

> *John 3:5-6 (NKJV) Jesus answered, "Most assuredly, I say to you, unless one is born of **water** and the **Spirit**, he cannot enter the kingdom of God." ⁶ That which is born of the flesh is flesh, and that which is born of the Spirit is spirit.*

Jesus is telling us the first birth is our physical birth, when we were born through our mothers' womb. In this scripture Jesus referred to this as *"born of water."* This first birth is our entry into the existence of this world. When we were in our mother's womb our life began as a seed in a water filled sack within our mother's womb. This is where we began to grow and develop. At a certain point, usually about nine months, we become mature enough as infants to graduate to the next step in life. Just prior to birth, the water filled sack breaks and water comes flowing out of the womb and the baby follows soon afterwards. When our life began as a seed, our being included a spirit, soul, and body.

As we have already learned we were all born with a sin nature because our natural father's seed was infected with sin. So, sin existed in us when we were born, because of Adam's sin. Obviously, every newborn infant did not violate God's laws while in the mother's womb. The baby didn't sin while he was in the womb, nor did the baby sin immediately when he came out of his mother's womb. This sin nature, that the baby was born with was not something the baby caused; but Adam caused it. We will not go into detail, but we can take comfort in that, the baby will not be judged and found guilty of sin until the baby grows, develops, and reaches an age of accountability. In other words, we can have confidence that those who die before reaching the age of accountability will spend eternity with God. Perhaps we could compare a baby's status with the first age of innocence. As such, in some ways the baby would be like that of Adam and Eve's original status of innocence.

> *Spiritual beings (angels and demons) can't be born again.*

Another point we learn from this scripture is that this new birth is only available to mankind. This new birth is not available to angels or demons because they were not born of water, meaning they are spirit beings not physical beings.

We also know they were created spirits, not spirits that were born, so they couldn't be "born again" if they were not born a first time. We also know that any other physical beings such as birds, fish, or other physical creatures can't be born again because they do not have a spirit. Man is the only physical being that has a spirit.

Now, this scripture says that unless one is born of water and of the Spirit, he cannot enter the kingdom of God. So, both births are required to enter the kingdom of God. This is where the second birth comes into the picture. Because every person **born of the flesh** is born with a sin nature, he is automatically condemned to death because of Adam's sin, which infected his seed. But now Jesus is saying that every person that is **born of the Spirit** is reborn with God's Seed. This is a game changer. God's Seed doesn't have sin or sin nature. God's Seed incorporates the very nature of God. So, when we are born-again of the Spirit, we receive the Life of God including His attributes, because just as we inherited the nature of Adam through his seed, now we inherit the nature of God through His Seed.

At our first birth (flesh) we inherit the nature of our natural father Adam, and now when we are born-again (spiritual), we inherit the nature of our spiritual Father, God. A primary benefit is that everyone born-again is forgiven of all their sins and saved by grace through faith in Jesus. We know this because He is implying that after we are born-again, we can enter the kingdom of God.

The second birth is spiritual. Jesus explains flesh gives birth to flesh and Spirit gives birth to spirit. Jesus is saying and clarifying that it is our spirit that is born again. Several things happen when we are born-again.

> *1 John 3:9 (NKJV) Whoever has been born of God does not sin, for His seed remains in him; and he cannot sin, because he has been born of God.*

We have already reviewed that when we are born in the flesh through our mother's womb we had a spirit, soul, and body and our spirit was dead to God because of Adam's sin, his seed infected with sin.

But now our spirit is born of God's Seed, and this scripture is a promise that His Seed will remain in us. He will not leave us or forsake us. Since God's Seed is in us, we cannot sin. That is why this scripture can boldly proclaim that we cannot sin anymore. Now through God, we are born again in the Spirit. Our spirit is born of God. Our spirit comes out of the womb of God! Our spirit-man becomes a new creation in Christ.

2 Corinthians 5:17 (NKJV) [17] *Therefore, if anyone is in Christ, he is a new creation; old things have passed away; behold, all things have become new.*

Let's analyze this scripture. Since we are reborn of God, we are a new creation (a new species). Old things have passed away is referring to our old life which has passed away and now our new life in God has begun.

To gain clarity of this reality let's summarize the history of the make-up of mankind.

1. God created the first Adam as a human being. Adam was unique from every other creature that God created, as man was made in the image and likeness of God. Man did not know sin and enjoyed a wonderful relationship with God.

2. The first Adam sinned in a manner that allowed sin to reign in his whole being. The result was death, and sin became part of his nature. When Adam's spirit died, he was dead to God because Adam terminated his relationship with God. The nature of Satan is sin and death. The first Adam's sin had infected his seed with the nature of sin, and that infected seed was of Satan and passed on to every person born in the flesh ever since. In other words, Adam's sin nature was inherited by every human being born.

3. The Last Adam (Jesus Christ) brought salvation to mankind. Our spirit is reborn of God, and we become a new creation. As a result, we are a child of God. The very Nature of God dwells in us. The Holy Spirit resides in our spirit! Throughout all parts of God's creation, mankind is the only being that can receive this incredible gift of salvation.

When we are born-again, we denounce our citizenship in this world and obtain our new citizenship in the kingdom of God.

In 1 John 4:4 we read "you are of God my little children." This means we are part of the very life of God. God's nature has been poured into our spirit, for we are of God. We are also children of God.

> Jesus said this is what we should rejoice in, that "**our name is written in the book of life**" which simply means we will live with Him for eternity.

When we are born again our spirit is made whole. Not only are all our sins forgiven, but our spirit also doesn't have a sin nature anymore. As a result, our spiritual relationship with God is restored to the same status that God intended for us from the beginning and our name is written in the book of life.

Our spirit-man is a new creation! We now possess the God filled life or zoe" life in our spirit. This is who we are, and it is important we receive the full revelation of what this means.

In some ways our spirit is just like our bodies in that our born-again spirit begins life as a newborn infant. In other words, our spirit requires nourishment and needs developing to grow and mature. As a natural baby, we are **dependent** on our mother to provide nourishment to our body when she feeds us and takes care of us. Similarly, as a baby in Christ, we can get nourishment in our spirit from the Word of God to grow and mature and we recognize that we are **dependent** on God to receive that nourishment.

> 1 Peter 1:23 (NKJV) [23] having been born again, not of corruptible seed but incorruptible, through the word of God which lives and abides forever,

Our spirit is reborn with an incorruptible and immortal Seed, which means our spirit cannot sin and as a result will live in eternity with God.

That is why we can stand before the throne of God as stated in Hebrews 4:16. Our spirit is righteous in His sight, and we will be righteous for eternity. When we are born-again the link from our spirit to God's throne is reconnected so that we can live the "zoe" life with Him. This scripture says our spirit is now born of an incorruptible seed which means the link or connection from our spirit to God will never be broken again and we will always be dependent on God, we know He is always faithful so we know we will live into eternity with Him.

The Holy Spirit Dwells Inside Our Spirit

Consider the depth of our status as a new creation. We are a new species; we belong to a different race. No other creature on earth or in heaven is born of God and has the very nature of God and the third Member of the Godhead dwelling inside their being! We are members of the Royal Family.

> John 14:16-17 (NKJV) [16] And I will pray the Father, and He will give you another Helper, that He may abide with you forever— [17] the Spirit of truth, whom the world cannot receive, because it neither sees Him nor knows Him; but you know Him, for **He dwells with you and will be in you.**

This scripture is so powerful. In this scripture Jesus is talking with His disciples just before His crucifixion and He is telling them He will be leaving but don't worry – it will get even better because He will send the Holy Spirit. The very Spirit of God dwells with us and is in us. Yes, the very same Spirit of God that was involved in creating the universe lives inside of us. What an incredible miracle. This new creature that our spirit has become is holy and so pure that the Spirit of God dwells inside of us.

> John 14:26 (NKJV) [26] But the Helper, the Holy Spirit, whom the Father will send in My name, He will teach you all things, and bring to your remembrance all things that I said to you.

He came to dwell inside of us to teach us all things. Stop and pause for a moment and consider this scripture. Do we truly believe this? He will teach us all that we need to know. It is so very important that we learn to allow our spirit to be king of our being or on the throne of our being because the Holy Spirit is willing to teach us and lead us in our victorious walk-through eternity.

How Do We Get Born-Again?

So how can we obtain this great salvation and who is eligible to receive it?

> *Romans 10:9 (NKJV)* [9] *that if you* **confess with your mouth** *the Lord Jesus and* **believe in your heart** *that God has raised Him from the dead, you will be saved.*

This is a two-step process.

1. Confess with your mouth that Jesus is Lord, and
2. Believe in your heart that God raised Jesus from the dead.

That's it! This is a free gift or grace that God has offered to everyone that follows these two steps. If you have not yet done this, you can do it right now.

It doesn't matter if you have been what the world would consider to be a "good person", or if the world considers you as an "evil person". You may go to church, you may tithe, you are nice to others, and are generally kind to others, or you may be an individual that everyone can easily identify as a sinner and you openly and boldly display outward signs of evil and sin. Both of these types of people are already judged and pronounced guilty of sin and condemned to death and will spend eternity in hell if they don't put their trust in Jesus Christ. This is because everyone is born with the sin nature, and everyone has sinned, regardless of their outward appearance to the world. It is not a matter of how much we may have sinned, or which sins we have committed. It doesn't matter which country you live in or what your background has been. The scripture simply says that all men have sinned and fallen short of the glory of God. Therefore, to receive salvation all you need to do is follow these two steps.

1. Confess with your mouth that Jesus is Lord and

2. Believe in your heart that God raised Jesus from the dead.; This gift from God is available to every man and woman on earth, if you follow these two steps.

If you have confessed Jesus as Lord and you believe in your heart that God raised Jesus from the dead, you are saved. This is how we are born-again. You are a new creature in Christ and your name is written in the book of life.

As we look into the elements of salvation, there is more information that will help individuals understand the benefits of this new life. We now know that Jesus came to save us but what did He save us from? Who can receive salvation and how does an individual receive salvation? We have already shared details about our legal right to salvation, but now let's consider more, such as what is the legal authority and method in which we can receive salvation? Was salvation possible for those in the Old Testament? If so, how was it different?

As we answer these questions let's start with what are we saved from?

Simply put, salvation means we are saved from our sin nature and the effects of sin.

CHAPTER 10

The Mechanics of Obtaining Salvation

As we consider the process of salvation there are three keywords that will help us to understand the mechanics that allow us to receive salvation. Let's look further into the Bible to get further revelation about these three words – grace, faith, and righteousness.

Saved by Grace Through Faith

> *Ephesians 2:8 (NKJV)* [8] *For **by grace you have been saved through faith**, and that not of yourselves; it is the gift of God,*

To obtain salvation is quick and simple and it's free. The Apostle Paul is very clear in this scripture that we are saved by grace through faith. It was not by our works or any work of our doing that we were saved. It is available by God's grace through faith. For the last 2,000 years there have been many religious people who have been hung up on the simplicity of salvation. God wants everyone to receive salvation, so He made it very simple for everyone to receive this gift.

We are going to explain the legal steps and requirements that Jesus went through for us, but our role is very simple – by grace we are saved. Grace is a gift from God.

*Romans 3:23-24 (NKJV) for all have sinned and fall short of the glory of God, [24] being **justified freely by His grace** through the redemption that is in Christ Jesus,*

This scripture tells us that we are justified by His grace. This grace is received in faith in Jesus Christ who is our righteousness.

> *What is this grace and how do we obtain grace?*

If we are saved by grace through faith what is this grace that the Apostle Paul is referring too? How do we have faith to obtain this grace? Why did I need this salvation?

To understand these two words, grace, and faith, and particularly from a biblical perspective, it will be helpful to first grasp the concept that God's focus toward mankind is based on His desire to have a loving relationship with us.

In 1 Corinthians chapter 12 and 14 the Apostle Paul is discussing spiritual gifts or grace. As Paul is explaining this grace or spiritual gifts he is interrupted by the "love" chapter 13, to talk about love. Love is a foundation of God's character. This grace or spiritual gifts that Paul is talking about is very important for us, but God also thought it was important that we understand that the basis of these gifts was love. So, in the middle of this teaching on spiritual gifts (grace) He pauses to tell us not to forget everything that needs to be bathed in love.

Therefore, our primary desire should also be to have a loving relationship with Him. Love should be our natural response because God's nature and character are founded in love, and we were made in His image according to His likeness. It will be helpful as we go through this section to keep our focus on the love of God. It will also be helpful to remember that God's nature and character didn't change from the Old Testament to the New Testament. He is the same God, and His character hasn't changed.

This is a key to understanding the pathway to eternal life with God and grasping more knowledge and understanding of God's character. Let's take a deeper look at grace and faith to obtain biblical perspectives of these words.

Grace

Like many words, grace can have multiple meanings or connotations. The grace of God can be as broad as describing the whole of God's activity towards man or as narrow as describing one specific segment of His activity toward man. An accurate and common definition of God's biblical grace is "God's unmerited favor toward man." As it states in Ephesians 2:8 grace is a gift from God. Grace is not earned, it's a gift.

The term grace is used in both the New and Old Testament. Many times, in the Old Testament grace more often refers to man giving unmerited favor to other men. The New Testament incorporates the term grace much more than the Old Testament. In the New Testament grace is most frequently used in reference to God's grace to man, rather than man's grace to man. But regardless, the theological concept of grace we are focused on in this section is the grace of God demonstrated towards men.

> *Genesis 6:8-9 (NKJV)* [8] *But **Noah found grace** in the eyes of the LORD.*
> *Noah Pleases God*
> [9] *This is the genealogy of Noah. Noah was a just man, perfect in his generations. Noah walked with God.*

This is an example in the Old Testament when Noah found God's grace. It then goes on to say he was a just man. He was considered a just man because he believed or trusted in God. The evidence of that is that it says he walked with God. Note that it doesn't say Noah was a perfect man, but he was considered just and that he walked with God. That implies he trusted God and believed in Him.

The Bible tells us that during the time of Noah, God was grieved because He saw the level of wickedness in the world, and He had to execute judgement to preserve the world and mankind. We all know this judgement came as a flood over all the earth. But Noah and his family were saved from this judgement because of Noah's belief and trust in the Lord, he found God's grace.

Another very good Old Testament example of grace was when God delivered the Israelites from the bondage of slavery in Egypt. Most people are all aware of the story when God released the plagues over Egypt and Pharaoh continued to harden his heart against God and the Israelites. While the plagues demonstrate God's power in judgment, the Passover demonstrates God's mercy and grace.

In Exodus chapter twelve, during the last plague, God provided a way for his people to be spared from judgement which was to be carried out in the death of the firstborn of all man and beast. The children of Israel were told by Moses to sacrifice a lamb and put its shed blood on the doorposts of their homes. The blood of that lamb represented life and the doorposts represented the entry to life. In other words, the shed blood of the lamb was a sacrifice to cover their sins and take the place of their death and be a **substitute** for the firstborn from each family. As God executed judgement on all of Egypt, it was God's grace that He passed over those homes that had the blood of the lamb on its doorposts. Their obedience showed they believed that God would save their life as He promised. This is an excellent example of God's grace to the children of Israel in the Old Testament because they believed and trusted Him that the blood of the lamb would cover them as a substitute for their death.

There are many other examples of grace in the Old Testament. In both the Old and New Testament sometimes the specific word grace is used and at other times it is the story that refers to the unmerited favor from God.

Now as we look in the New Testament, we will see many more uses of the term grace and in more applications. During this review keep in mind that the basic definition we are focusing on is related to the concept that grace is the unmerited favor of God, or in other words, it's a gift from God. Everyone likes to get gifts especially when they are free.

But let's now focus on the most important gift in all of history. It's the gift of life. Specifically, our resurrected life.

> *Ephesians 2:8 (NKJV)* [8] *For **by grace you have been saved through faith**, and that not of yourselves; it is the gift of God,*

> *Romans 5:15 (NKJV)* [15] *But the free gift is not like the offense. For if by the one man's offense many died, much more the **grace of God** and the gift by the grace of the one Man, Jesus Christ, abounded to many.*

Again, an important key is to remember that God is love and He loves every person ever born on earth and desires that everyone accepts His grace so they may have eternal life with Him.

God gave each of us our own will, so that we can decide the destiny of our future and our home for eternity. He has provided the Way (Jesus) to eternal life for every person if we choose to live eternally with Him. But remember, that decision must be made before we leave our earthly body or in other words, before we physically die.

> *Grace is a gift from God. Grace comes as a result of God's love to mankind.*

The specific grace or gift we are referring to is our resurrected life. God gave us His righteousness so that we could be resurrected with Jesus and be with Him for eternity.

God knew that everyone has need of a Savior to restore life to as many that choose Him and choose to enter His Kingdom. He showed us grace by giving us the law and sacrifices to point us to our Savior. Many people today still try to meet the requirements of the Mosaic law and continue trying to be good enough to receive salvation or be accepted by God through their own good works. But even God has told us we can't meet the requirements of the law ourselves.

> *John 1:17 (NKJV)* *17 For the law was given through Moses, but grace and truth came through Jesus Christ.*

The Apostle John lays out two options available to us but only one of these provides for salvation. This gift or grace that comes from Jesus Christ is simply God's love for us.

To summarize, grace from God comes in many forms because He loves us so much and desires that we have the best, so He gives us many good gifts. But the grace we are specifically talking about here is the grace needed for our salvation. It is the gift of righteousness that allows us to be holy in the eyes of God.

Righteousness

> *Romans 10:1-4 (NKJV)* *1 Brethren, my heart's desire and prayer to God for Israel is that they may be saved. 2 For I bear them witness that they have a zeal for God, but not according to knowledge. 3 For they being ignorant of **God's righteousness**, and seeking to establish **their own righteousness**, have not submitted to the **righteousness of God**. 4 For Christ is the end of the law for righteousness to everyone who believes.*

Biblical righteousness of God means we have the ability to stand in the presence of God without the sense of sin consciousness. When God created Adam, we know that He created him as a righteous being because afterward God looked at Adam and said this is very good. We also know that God had a close friendship with Adam and Eve because they walked and talked in the garden each afternoon. God couldn't/wouldn't do that if Adam and Eve weren't righteous. We know that God is holy and righteous, and sin is unrighteous.

That means that for mankind to be able to dwell in God's presence he must be declared righteous. 1 John 5:17 says "all unrighteousness is sin…." So, the question becomes how do we obtain this righteousness if we have a sin nature?

> One of man's basic needs is to obtain the righteousness of God. The righteousness of God is much different than the righteousness of man.

As we have discussed, man does not have the ability to obtain **Godly righteousness** on his own merits. It is simply not possible for man to completely remove the nature of sin from his life without God's help. We have all been through times in our life when we try so hard to be free from sin on our own. But it can just end up bringing guilt and condemnation, because in essence our attempts to obtain righteousness are only **self-righteousness**. And self-righteousness or man's righteousness will never be sufficient to qualify for salvation.

Unrighteousness

In Romans 1:18 -32 the Apostle Paul is **speaking of the Gentiles** and Paul expresses God's anger against all sinful, wicked people that suppress the truth, and He goes on to describe some of their sinful acts with an emphasis on their sexual sins and unnatural desires. He also makes it clear that God has revealed Himself to the Gentiles from the beginning and they have a means of salvation.

> *Romans 1:21 (NLT)* [21] *Yes, they knew God, but they wouldn't worship him as God or even give him thanks. And they began to think up foolish ideas of what God was like. As a result, their minds became dark and confused.*

During this dialogue, these scriptures tell us that even the wicked people know about God. Many scriptures including this dialogue confirm that God reveals Himself through nature. But they refused to worship Him or give Him thanks. Many of their sinful acts are revealed here with an emphasis on sexual sins. However, they made plans or ideas in their own minds to avoid the real truth. Today in our society, this is referred to as "their own truth," but in reality, they are only deceiving themselves with lies. There is only one truth and that can only be confirmed in the Word of God.

> *Romans 1:32 (NLT)* [32] *They know God's justice requires that those who do these things deserve to die, yet they do them anyway. Worse yet, they encourage others to do them, too.*

He finishes this dialogue in this verse by stating they inherently know truth but refuse to change their ways and turn to God.

Then Paul continued in Romans 2:1-38. Paul changes his focus and is **speaking to the Jews** and says they are just as bad, and they don't even have an excuse because God gave them the law and the sacrifices. He explains that the Jews do have benefits as a chosen people but in the end, God does not show favoritism.

Romans 2:29 (NLT) ²⁹ No, a true Jew is one whose heart is right with God. And true circumcision is not merely obeying the letter of the law; rather, it is a change of heart produced by God's Spirit. And a person with a changed heart seeks praise from God, not from people.

Paul continues His dialogue to the Jews by revealing their sins. They use God's laws to judge others of their sins, but they commit the same sins themselves.

Both of these dialogues describe the **un-righteousness** of mankind. This is the power of sin. The Jews had the law of God and a more complete revelation of God which had many advantages but that didn't release them or the Gentiles from judgment of sin. In other words, we are judged for sin regardless of our level of knowledge. Both groups are responsible for their own sins and will be held accountable for their sins.

Romans 3:19-20 (NLT) Obviously, the law applies to those to whom it was given, for its purpose is to keep people from having excuses, and to show that the entire world is guilty before God. ²⁰ For no one can ever be made right with God by doing what the law commands. The law simply shows us how sinful we are.

This scripture simply summarizes that all people in the world have sinned and will be declared guilty of sin if they don't receive the help of a Savior. These scriptures also verify that all mankind is aware of their **unrighteousness** at least with some level of awareness so ignorance is not an excuse for sin.

1 John 1:9 (NKJV) ⁹ If we confess our sins, He is faithful and just to forgive us our sins and to cleanse us from all unrighteousness.

> *2 Corinthians 5:21 (NKJV)* ²¹ *For He made Him who knew no sin to be sin for us, that we might become the righteousness of God in Him.*

Let's consider another view of unrighteousness.

> *Hebrews 3:17 - 4:2 (NKJV)* ¹⁷ *Now with whom was He angry forty years? Was it not with those who sinned, whose corpses fell in the wilderness?* ¹⁸ *And to whom did He swear that they would not enter His rest, but to those who did not obey?* ¹⁹ *So we see that they could not enter because of* ***unbelief.***

This scripture says they couldn't enter because of their unbelief. Simply not believing God is sin or unrighteousness. Many people think if they don't lie, cheat, and steal they meet the requirements. But this scripture says that "*unbelieve*" or not trusting in God, is sin.

Self-Righteousness

So, we have learned that all of mankind is guilty of sin, and we also know that all sin is unrighteous, and that unrighteous people can't enter the Kingdom of God or fellowship with God. We also just learned that all of mankind is aware of this fact.

The Bible tells us that some wicked people harden their hearts and just refuse to acknowledge God's goodness and their purpose to focus on their own thoughts and evil desires.

But there are many other people throughout the world that recognize and distinguish the difference between the goodness of God and evil thoughts and desires. These are people that we recognize as good people. They can be mild mannered, kind, and considerate of others. They can give to the poor, take others in with kindness. They perceive or understand that evil deeds have negative consequences, and therefore they purposely do what is right in their own eyes. They generally aim to be nice and kind to others. While all of these are good things and honorable deeds, they still fall short of God's standard of righteousness.

> *Philippians 3:9 (NKJV) 9 and be found in Him, not having my own righteousness, which is from the law, but that which is through faith in Christ, the righteousness which is from God by faith;*

This scripture separates people into two groups.
1. *Those people focused on their own righteousness from the law.*
2. *Those people focused on righteousness of God through faith.*

Our own righteousness is simply self-righteousness. Let's consider self-righteousness and why is it not good enough? Let's first consider the "self" in self-righteousness. It is all about self. It comes from within us and it's about ourselves. Self is a reference to our soul. Let's go back to the tree of knowledge of good and evil. This knowledge of good and evil comes from our own soul. It's not the same as knowledge that comes from God. It is self-generated, and we know that we can't deliver ourselves from evil on our own. Even people that are born-again can fall into this cycle of self-righteousness.

> *Isaiah 64:6 (NKJV) But we are all like an unclean thing,*
> *And all our righteousnesses are like filthy rags;*
> *We all fade as a leaf,*
> *And our iniquities, like the wind,*
> *Have taken us away.*

This scripture is simply saying *"**our righteousness are** like filthy rags."* The focus here is on self.

The Pharisees give us another good example of self-righteousness. They thought they were good enough to meet the requirements of the Mosaic law. But we know from the Bible and from our own experiences that sin is in our nature, and we can't meet the requirements of the law on our own. Any attempts to do so are self-righteousness.

Godly-Righteousness

> *Romans 3:21 (NKJV) ²¹ But now the righteousness of God apart from the law is revealed, being witnessed by the Law and the Prophets,*

The word righteousness as used above in the Greek is dikaiosune, Strong's #1343. It is described in Vine's dictionary as, "the character or quality of being right or just"; it was formerly spelled "rightwiseness," which more clearly expresses the meaning. It is used to denote an attribute of God, the context of which shows that "the righteousness of God" means essentially the same as His faithfulness, or truthfulness, that which is consistent with His own nature and promises.

> *Romans 3:22 (NLT) ²² We are made right with God by placing our faith in Jesus Christ. And this is true for everyone who believes, no matter who we are.*

The good news is that Jesus came to solve that problem for us. What we need to know is that we need faith to obtain Godly righteousness. The law and the sacrificial system made that perfectly clear to us. We need the help of a **Substitute** to allow us the opportunity to obtain this Godly righteousness. This Substitution is a gift from God to us. So, to further explain Godly righteousness we need to move on and discuss the next keyword.

Faith

Now that we have a more complete understanding of Godly righteousness and grace, let's grasp an understanding of faith, which is the pathway to obtain this grace (gift from God). Many books have been written about faith and our purpose here is to provide a simple overview of faith and how we are to obtain it.

> *Hebrews 11:6 (NKJV)* ⁶ *But without faith it is impossible to please Him, for he who comes to God must believe that He is, and that He is a rewarder of those who diligently seek Him.*

This is a good eye-opener for many people. "*without faith it is impossible to please God.*" Nobody wants to have God displeased with them. So, let's pay close attention to the definition of faith and how we can obtain faith. Let's start with some Old Testament examples. This helps to validate that God has always been the same loving God throughout history.

> *Hebrews 11:7 (NKJV)* ⁷ ***By faith*** *Noah, being divinely warned of things not yet seen, moved with godly fear, prepared an ark for the saving of his household, by which he condemned the world and became heir of the righteousness which is according to faith.*

> *Hebrews 11:8 (NKJV)* ⁸ ***By faith*** *Abraham obeyed when he was called to go out to the place which he would receive as an inheritance. And he went out, not knowing where he was going.*

> *Hebrews 11:11 (NKJV)* ¹¹ ***By faith*** *Sarah herself also received strength to conceive seed, and she bore a child when she was past the age, because she judged Him faithful who had promised.*

Hebrews 11:17 (NKJV) ¹⁷ ***By faith*** *Abraham, when he was tested, offered up Isaac, and he who had received the promises offered up his only begotten son,*

Hebrews 11:23 (NKJV) ²³ ***By faith*** *Moses, when he was born, was hidden for three months by his parents, because they saw he was a beautiful child; and they were not afraid of the king's command.*

Hebrews 11:31 (NKJV) ³¹ ***By faith*** *the harlot Rahab did not perish with those who did not believe, when she had received the spies with peace.*

This is a just sampling of Old Testament examples in the book of Hebrews that shows examples of people that walked in faith. God has always worked through men and women of faith. It can easily be seen that "*by faith*" is the theme. Noah prepared the ark because he believed what God told him about the coming flood. Note that this happened before God gave the law to Moses. Sarah and Abraham are also examples of people that walked in faith before the law came. Many other examples are given about heroes of faith after Moses but before Jesus.

Hebrews 11:39-40 (NKJV) And all these, having obtained a good testimony through faith, did not receive the promise, ⁴⁰ *God having provided something better for us, that they should not be made perfect apart from us.*

This scripture says all of these received a good testimony, but none of them received the promise. What is the promise they didn't receive? Perhaps we need to ask what or who their faith was in first?

> *In God's economy He accounts our faith as righteousness. This is a core element to our salvation.*

190

All these heroes of faith were trusting God. They believed God loved them and they trusted Him with their life.

> *Romans 4:3 (NKJV) [3] For what does the Scripture say? "Abraham believed God, and it was **accounted to him for righteousness.**"*

> *Romans 4:5 (NKJV) [5] But to him who does not work but believes on Him who justifies the ungodly, **his faith is accounted for righteousness,***

> *Romans 4:6-8 (NKJV) just as David also describes the blessedness of the man to whom **God imputes righteousness apart from works:***
> *[7] "Blessed are those whose lawless deeds are forgiven,*
> *And whose sins are covered;*
> *[8] Blessed is the man to whom the LORD shall not impute sin."*

Here we see three scriptures that show the benefit of faith. God accounts faith as righteousness. This is a core biblical foundation. These heroes are examples of faith, and the Bible tells us their faith is credited to them as righteousness.

From an accounting perspective these Old Testament saints have been issued a credit to their account for righteousness.

> *Romans 4:13 (NKJV) [13] For the promise that he would be the heir of the world was not to Abraham or to his seed through the law, but through the righteousness of faith.*

This scripture is referring to the promise God gave to Abraham that through Abraham all the nations of the world would be blessed. This is saying that the promise was not to come through the natural seed of

Abraham or through the law but through the **righteousness of faith**. We obtain righteousness through faith.

> *Romans 4:18-19 (NKJV)* ⁸ *who, contrary to hope, in hope believed, so that he became the father of many nations, according to what was spoken, "So shall your descendants be."* ¹⁹ *And not being weak in faith, he did not consider his own body, already dead (since he was about a hundred years old), and the deadness of Sarah's womb.*

> *Romans 4:22 (NKJV)* ²² *And therefore "it was accounted to him for righteousness."*

Let's follow the storyline – God told Abraham that through his descendants all the nations would be blessed. The problem was that Abraham was an old man – 100 years old and Sarah his wife was 90 years old. They were childless and in the natural it was impossible for them to have children. But Abraham believed God that it would happen, and God counted Abraham's belief or faith in God's promise to him as righteousness.

What is Faith?

> *Hebrews 11:1 (NKJV)* ¹ *Now faith is the substance of things hoped for, the evidence of things not seen.*

This scripture separates faith and hope. Many people don't understand the difference between the two. According to this scripture hope comes before faith. Hope is very important.

Hope

> *Jeremiah 29:11 (NKJV)* ¹¹ *For I know the thoughts that I think toward you, says the LORD, thoughts of peace and not of evil, to give you a future and a* ***hope****.*

Proverbs 13:12 (NKJV) [12] **Hope** *deferred makes the heart sick, But when the desire comes, it is a tree of life.*

Psalms 42:11 (NKJV) [11] *Why are you cast down, O my soul? And why are you disquieted within me?*
Hope *in God;*
For I shall yet praise Him,
The help of my countenance and my God.

Romans 15:13 (NKJV) [13] *Now may the God of* **hope** *fill you with all joy and peace in believing, that you may abound in hope by the power of the Holy Spirit.*

Romans 5:3-5 (NKJV) And not only that, but we also glory in tribulations, knowing that tribulation produces perseverance; [4] *and perseverance, character; and character,* **hope.** [5] *Now* **hope** *does not disappoint, because the love of God has been poured out in our hearts by the Holy Spirit who was given to us.*

This is a small sampling of the many hope scriptures in the Bible. God is telling us that hope is a very important aspect to desire in our lives. Godly hope is envisioning the positive result of a desire for something that gives glory to God.

Faith

Now faith can have different applications. We can have faith that when we turn a light switch to the on position the light will come on. We have developed faith in this process because we have done it many times, so we have a confident expectation that the light will come on. But the faith we are looking at is Bible faith – the God kind of faith. This faith is based on God's Word.

> *Hope can be defined as a joyful, confident expectation.*

All the faith heroes we looked at had faith in something that God said. They had a joyful, confident, expectation (hope) in what God said would come to pass. In other words, they believed what God said.

> *Hebrews 12:2 (NKJV) ² looking unto **Jesus, the author and finisher of our faith**, who for the joy that was set before Him endured the cross, despising the shame, and has sat down at the right hand of the throne of God.*

> *Jesus is the originator or founder of faith. When we seek and desire faith, we need to begin our search the Bible with Jesus as our focus.*

This seems to be a good place to begin considering faith. We see here that Jesus is the author and finisher of our faith. Another way to say this is Jesus is the originator and perfecter of our faith.

As the founder of faith there is nobody more qualified to learn from than Jesus. He perfected our faith! As we continue our review, we will draw from scriptures to learn more about faith. *"The Word was made flesh"* is speaking of Jesus.

> *Romans 10:17 (NKJV) ¹⁷ So then faith comes by hearing, and hearing by the word of God.*

The more we focus on His Word and particularly the good news about Jesus Christ, then the more faith we receive. That is because He did so much for us. The more we understand what He did for us, the more faith we have in Him.

We also learn from Hebrews 12:2 that a motivator to assist Jesus or strengthen His endurance was the joy that He imagined from sitting at the right hand of His Father again, and spending eternity with us. Jesus was fully aware of the intensity of the mental, emotional and physical anguish and suffering He was about to experience at the cross. But rather than dwelling on how hard it was going to be or questioning Himself – can I really do this; He put His focus and paid attention to remember why He is going to the cross. We learn that His intentions were focused on two primary goals.

1. To do the will of His Father.

2. Complete the process to reconcile us back into His presence for eternity.

The point is, to keep focus on your purpose, not the challenges you may face. In His spirit Jesus knew what He was called to do. In His mind, He accepted, processed and reasoned with His calling, and aligned His will with His Fathers will. Then He purposed to use His emotions of joy to strengthen Himself.

Many times, people do just the opposite and focus their attention on the challenges they face and allow their emotions including fear to lead their decisions.

> Romans 1:17 (NLT) *¹⁷ This Good News tells us how **God makes us right in his sight**. This is accomplished from start to finish by faith. As the Scriptures say, "It is through faith that a righteous person has life."*

This scripture in the NLT translation sets the stage for us. The phrase "God makes us right in His sight" appears eight times in Romans and has roots in the Old Testament. This scripture is not saying that God makes us good people. Rather this is a legal statement of position. It means God puts us in the right legal standing before God. What is it that puts us in right legal standing with God? It's our faith.

> It is through faith that we are considered righteous before God.

This is a core component of our salvation, and it is how we receive our new life as a believer. Faith is believing that God is who He said He is. It is based on believing that He did what He said He would do to save us from our sins.

In summary we are saying that we believe or have faith that Jesus died for my sins and was resurrected because He was sinless and that as I believe in Him and what He did for me, God accounts the righteousness of Jesus to my account. In other words, my belief or faith is that His righteousness has become my righteousness.

What About Old Testament Believers?

Now we know from reading the Bible that there are people in the Old Testament that we will see in heaven, and we will be with them for eternity. What is their pathway to eternal life? Is the salvation of Old Testament saints different than the New Testament saints?

There is a difference in timing but that doesn't mean salvation was not available in the Old Testament. We have already seen that there were people declared righteous in the Old Testament, but they were under the old covenant.

We know that God spoke to people in the Old Testament in various different ways throughout the different ages, worlds, or time periods.

> *Hebrews 1:1-2 (NKJV) God, who at various times and in various ways spoke in time past to the fathers by the*

prophets, ² has in these last days spoken to us by His Son, whom He has appointed heir of all things, through whom also He made the worlds;

This scripture is telling us that God spoke to people throughout the ages, through angels, a burning bush, dreams, visions, or even a direct voice from heaven.

But ever since Adam sinned, the way man approached God has always been the same – by grace through faith.

Hebrews 11:39-40 (NKJV) And all these, having obtained a good testimony through faith, did not receive the promise, ⁴⁰ God having provided something better for us, that they should not be made perfect apart from us.

Old Testament believers heard from God, and as they believed Him, He considered them righteous. But there was no possibility for their spirit to be raised to life because the sacrificial Lamb had not yet come to earth to make provision for them. Because of their faith in Him they will receive the promise in due time.

But let's look at those who did not believe.

*Hebrews 3:17 - 4:2 (NKJV) ¹⁷ Now with whom was He angry forty years? Was it not with those who sinned, whose corpses fell in the wilderness? ¹⁸ And to whom did He swear that they would not enter His rest, but to those who did not obey? ¹⁹ So we see that they could not enter in **because of unbelief**.*

In this scripture we see the other side of this picture. After Moses led the Jews out of Egypt, they did not believe or trust the Lord or put their **dependence** on the Lord. In this example, when Moses sent out the 12 spies to survey the land and the people. When they returned, ten of the twelve spies came back with a negative report as they viewed the men in the promise land as giants and saw themselves as grasshoppers in comparison. God had told them He would go before them and give them this promised land. They didn't believe God that they could defeat the giants, which may have been true if they had to go to battle on their own. However, God told them that He would go before them and defeat the giants. They did not believe Him or trust Him or **depend** on Him. In other words, they were thinking and anticipating that they would have had to go to war against the giants independently from God. Their unbelief was accounted to them as sin and unrighteousness and consequently they all died in the wilderness because of their unbelief. Only the two spies, (Joshua and Caleb) came back with faith and believing God that He would give them the victory. These two believed, and therefore entered the promise land.

It is interesting to note that the author of Hebrews goes on to say in Hebrew 4:2 "*the gospel was preached to them as well as to us*". He is referring to those who did not mix the gospel (good news) with faith in God. Therefore, those that did not believe, died in the wilderness because of their unbelief and those that did believe, lived and entered into the promise land.

Let's compare an example of the Old Testament Gospel with the same example preached in the New Testament.

> *Deuteronomy 30:14 (NKJV)* ¹⁴ *But the word is very near you, in your mouth and in your heart, that you may do it.*

> *Romans 10:8-10 (NKJV) But what does it say? "The word is near you, in your mouth and in your heart" (that is, the word of faith which we preach):* ⁹ *that if you confess with your mouth the Lord Jesus and believe in your heart that*

God has raised Him from the dead, you will be saved. [10] For with the heart one believes unto righteousness, and with the mouth confession is made unto salvation.

These scriptures both showing us salvation was available in the Old and New Testament and the same two simple steps are required to receive it. They both require that we believe in our heart which is defining faith, trusting and being dependent on God. In the previous verses of Deuteronomy we get a prerequisite requirement saying *....if you believe with all your heart and soul...* Then it also requires that we confess it or speak it out.

The coming Messiah, the Way was prophesied throughout the Old Testament. Those who were looking for God and listening to God, knew that there was a Savior (Messiah) that was coming. God requires that we have faith. He desires that we believe in Him, and that we put our trust in Him, and we depend on Him.

Hebrews 11:6 (NKJV) [6] But without faith it is impossible to please Him, for he who comes to God must believe that He is, and that He is a rewarder of those who diligently seek Him.

This is a bold statement that it is impossible to please God without faith. There were many Old Testament saints that did have faith. The faith we are talking about is believing that He is, and that He is a rewarder of those who diligently seek Him. We see the summary of some Old Testament heroes that had this faith in Hebrews chapters eleven and twelve.

How did Abraham receive righteousness? He believed in the Lord. Another way of saying this is that Abraham trusted the Lord. That means he had to be **dependent** on the Lord. As we discussed when Adam sinned, he gave up his **dependance** on the Lord, and exchanged it for his

independence from God. Abraham did the opposite of Adam. Abraham believed in the Lord, he trusted in the Lord, and was therefore **dependent** on Him.

> *Galatians 3:6-8 (NKJV) just as Abraham "believed God, and it was accounted to him for righteousness." ⁷ Therefore know that only those who are of faith are sons of Abraham. ⁸ And the Scripture, foreseeing that God would justify the Gentiles by faith,* **preached the gospel to Abraham** *beforehand, saying, "In you all the nations shall be blessed."*

Galatians starts by repeating that Abraham *"believed God and it was accounted to him as righteousness."* These verses describe the situation further. God preached the gospel (good news of the coming Messiah) to Abraham about 2,000 years before the birth of Jesus. In fact, every book in the Old Testament prophesied about the coming Messiah. The gospel is the good news that Jesus would come and provide salvation to many through faith. Abraham's faith, trust, or dependence in the Lord was accounted to him as righteousness. This promise was not only to Abraham but to anyone who believes, trusts and is dependent on the Lord.

> *Hebrews 11:7 (NKJV) ⁷ By faith Noah, being divinely warned of things not yet seen, moved with godly fear, prepared an ark for the saving of his household, by which he condemned the world and became heir of the righteousness which is according to faith.*

Noah was another Old Testament believer. God warned him of the flood that was coming. In the natural it had never rained. In fact, there was nothing in the natural that would indicate a flood was coming. Can you imagine how Noah felt when he explained to his neighbors why he was building an ark? Nonetheless Noah believed God's Word and as a result he became an heir of righteousness which is according to his faith.

Hebrews 11:4 (NKJV) ⁴ *By faith Abel offered to God a more excellent sacrifice than Cain, through which he obtained witness that he was righteous, God testifying of his gifts; and through it he being dead still speaks.*

Here we see that by faith Abel offered a more excellent sacrifice and as a result he obtained witness that he was righteous.

Hebrews 11:30-31 (NKJV) By faith the walls of Jericho fell down after they were encircled for seven days. ³¹ *By faith the harlot Rahab did not perish with those who did not believe, when she had received the spies with peace.*

Even though Rahab was a harlot she did not perish because of her faith, but all the others who did not believe, perished or were killed.

We can see a recurring theme in these few examples of Old Testament saints, that righteousness comes because of faith and trusting God and depending on God for life.

We can summarize from all these examples in the Old Testament there were many individuals in the Old Testament that had faith in God, and it was accounted to them as righteousness, and they received God's grace. Likewise, we see the results of individuals in the Old Testament that did not believe or trust in God.

Now, we can see that righteousness was obtained through faith in God. This faith is referring to our **trust or dependance on God**. We can conclude that Old and New Testament believers are saved by grace through faith. The difference is that Old Testament believers were under the old covenant which was before Jesus offered Himself on the cross.

To further explain, there were many Old Testament saints that had faith in God that He would provide salvation through a Savoir (the Messiah) and that Savoir was God Himself. In other words, there were Old Testament saints that put their trust or dependence in God for salvation, but their physical bodies died prior to the death, burial, and resurrection of Jesus Christ.

So, since the time of their physical death, because of their faith in Him, they are sleeping in Abraham's bosom awaiting their full salvation. Other people in the Old Testament that did not put their trust or dependance in God are awaiting final judgement on the tormenting side of Hades which is the second death.

Those of us that are under the New Covenant are similar but different. Let's explain. When Jesus came to earth in the likeness of man He provided for the full salvation of all mankind at His death, burial, and resurrection. That includes New and Old Testament saints, meaning those who put their trust in Him.

So, anyone that was physically alive on earth that put their trust or dependance on Jesus after Pentecost and was born-again is saved. That means that while we are physically alive on earth, we receive this salvation. The day of Pentecost marks the beginning of the Church Age. The Bible describes the Church Age as the period from the day of Pentecost to the day of the rapture.

CHAPTER 11

Three phases of Salvation

As we approach this chapter regarding the three phases of salvation it is vital that we begin with understanding that the death, burial, resurrection, and ascension of Jesus Christ is complete. Jesus has completed all provisions that are required for our complete salvation.

These three phases of salvation are intended to give us authority over the penalty, the power, and the presence of sin in all aspects of our life. Remember it is sin that separates us from God and causes death.

Salvation is provided to us through Jesus Christ and is available to us in three phases. Each phase can be related to part of our being or perhaps we should say it brings emphasis towards each of the three parts of our being.

1. Spirit – Justification
2. Soul – Sanctification
3. Body - Glorification

	Three Phases of Salvation		
who	spirit	soul	body
phase	justification	sanctification	glorification
what	saved from the **penalty** of sin	saved from the **power** of sin	saved from the **presence** of sin
when	**past** when we are born-again	**present** throughout our life on earth	**future** at the first resurrection
how	a one-time experience of forgiveness for all sins. Our spirit is raised from death to life. Holy Spirit dwells in us.	continual process of renewing our mind and cleansing our soul.	transformation of our physical body into our eternal body.

The chart below identifies the who, what, when and how of the three phases of salvation. [Diagram 6]

Justification

What is justification? As we continue to understand the impact and the effect of what Jesus did for us on the cross it will be important to review the meaning of a few words beginning with justification. Justification is an act of God whereby He recognizes and declares a sinner to be righteous because of that sinner's faith in Jesus Christ. We understand that the penalty for sin is death. We know that Jesus died as a Substitute for our sins and now through faith we are justified, or declared righteous, at the moment of our salvation.

Justified or Justification is a legal term meaning; to render just, or to be declared righteous. It is a verdict or a decision, ruling, or judgement. It is a reason or explanation from a judge to legally declare a person righteous. During a hearing or trial, the judge will hear and observe the evidence submitted to the court, and after reviewing the evidence the judge declares the defendant guilty or not guilty. If the judge determines the individual not guilty, then the individual is declared to be justified before the court and the charges are dismissed.

Justification only needs to be declared once. After the individual has been declared not guilty or justified the effect of that verdict is that the individual is considered righteous.

Righteousness is the result of being declared innocent or not guilty. In other words, you become or are established to be righteous when you are justified.

Not-guilty vs innocent – Many people assume these two terms have the same meaning, but they can be different. Innocent means that the person did not commit the offense they have been charged with. Not guilty on the other hand could mean the person is innocent but it could also mean there was not sufficient evidence to convict the person of that offense. However, a verdict or declaration of not guilty or innocent can have the same effect. Either declaration (not guilty or innocent) can result in the person being justified.

Much of the foundation of the judicial system in the United States has been based on biblical principles. As such in our courts we generally do not consider or declare a person innocent. Rather our courts will declare a person guilty or not guilty. Not guilty is a lower standard than innocent. In other words, a person may have committed an offense but because of some reason the evidence was not sufficient to declare the individual guilty or there may have been some other extenuating circumstances.

This is the situation in our spiritual justification. We know that Jesus was sinless – meaning He was innocent of sin, therefore at His judgement Jesus was declared not-guilty. All the rest of us as human beings on the other hand, are all guilty of sin. But as we believe in faith that Jesus died as our Substitute, we as a result have been declared not guilty and we are considered justified which makes us righteous in Christ.

> *Romans 5:18 (NKJV) ¹⁸ Therefore, as through one man's offense judgment came to all men, resulting in condemnation, even so through one Man's righteous act the free gift came to all men, resulting in **justification of life**.*

We see our definitions used in this scripture. Adam, who was representing all of mankind was judged and declared guilty of his sin, and he was sentenced to death. His spirit died immediately, and his body was gradually decaying or dying. Adam's sin and death was passed on to all mankind and we were all affected or impacted in the same way.

Jesus is Our Substitute

We can recognize two things that happened at the cross and at Jesus' judgement.

1. The Last Adam, Jesus Christ, lived a sinless life and offered His life for our sins on the cross. Jesus took on our sins and paid the penalty for our sins through suffering and dying on the cross for our sins. In His death, he paid the price for our sins. He offered to give His life for us, as our Substitute.

2. He was also judged for His own life and was found sinless. Therefore, at His judgement He was declared not guilty. His judgement declared Him to be justified or made right. He was righteous in God's eyes because He was sinless; in being sinless He fulfilled all the requirements of the law.

In summary, Jesus' death was for our sins, not His. He also took on judgement for our sinful life and was sentenced to death and He fulfilled the law. Jesus was also judged for His own sinless life and declared not guilty because He fulfilled the law.

Jesus was resurrected from death because Death didn't have jurisdiction to take His life because Jesus was sinless. We can recognize what happened at Jesus' judgement. Death could not take Him because Death didn't have jurisdiction because Jesus was sinless.

Therefore, Jesus (last Adam) was a representative of mankind, just like the first Adam was a representative of mankind, Jesus' judgement could be passed on to all of mankind through faith in Him. [Diagram 7]

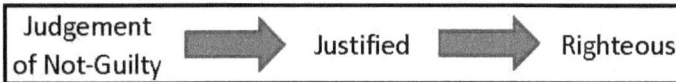

| Judgement of Not-Guilty | ➡ | Justified | ➡ | Righteous |

Justification took place immediately in our spirit when;

1. we openly confessed or spoke out that we acknowledge that we are sinners, and

2. we accepted and believed in our heart that Jesus died for our sins as our Substitute. In faith we can identify with His death, so that we can be set free from the penalty of sin.

Let's look at a few scriptures referencing the justification and righteousness we are all eligible to receive.

> Romans 3:21-24 (NKJV) But now the righteousness of God apart from the law is revealed, being witnessed by the Law and the Prophets, [22] even the righteousness of God, through faith in Jesus Christ, to all and on all who believe. For there is no difference; [23] for all have sinned and fall short of the glory of God, [24] being **justified freely by His grace** through the redemption that is in Christ Jesus,

*2 Corinthians 5:21 (NKJV) [21] For He made Him who knew no sin to be sin for us, that we might become **the righteousness of God** in Him.*

*Romans 5:1 (NKJV) [1] Therefore, having been **justified by faith**, we have peace with God through our Lord Jesus Christ,*

We can see in these scriptures and throughout the Bible a common theme. Through faith in Jesus Christ, we are justified and made righteous so that we can stand and be in right standing before the throne of God.

When Jesus (a sinless man) was nailed to the cross He took all the sins of the world upon Himself. As a sinless man, He was already innocent and righteous, and therefore death could not take Him because death had no legal authority. Jesus had full legal authority over death.

Remember this is not intended as a display of God's power but a statement of His legal authority because He was sinless. He took on our sins upon Himself and offered up His life as He was crucified on behalf of our sins. Jesus willfully became our Substitute and was crucified for our sins, (not His sins). He paid the penalty for our sins through death, so that we could be justified and made righteous before the throne of God.

> *The penalty for sin is death. Jesus took on our sins and died for us. He is our Substitute!*

Now remember we reviewed that because of Adam's sin all mankind was declared guilty of sin and was sentenced to death. But now because of an innocent man's death (Last Adam) all of mankind is eligible to be declared innocent or justified. Jesus is the perfect sacrifice – the Lamb of God. Again, as we discussed Jesus did this for us. And He has made this gift (grace) available to all of mankind.

John 5:24 (NKJV) [24] *"Most assuredly, I say to you, he who hears My word and believes in Him who sent Me has everlasting life, and shall **not come into judgment**, but has passed from death into life.*

John 6:47 (NKJV) [47] *Most assuredly, I say to you, he who believes in Me has everlasting life.*

Jesus is speaking in these two verses and making it clear that if we believe in Him, we will have eternal life. Because of what He did for us we won't experience the judgement that He experienced for us. Our spirit will pass from death to life because we are justified, and consequently our spirit is righteous.

When the first Adam sinned, his spirit immediately died as he passed from life to death. Now when we believe in Jesus Christ, the process is reversed, and our spirit passes from death to life.

God made the rules in the beginning and allowed Adam to choose life or death in the garden. When Adam chose to be **independent** of God, he chose death because Adam thought he could succeed in his life without God and still be just like God. As much as it saddened God, He had to keep His word to allow this to happen and watch mankind be fatally infected by sin. The only way that God could reverse the effect of Adam's decision and give life back to man's spirit was to send His Son, Jesus as a perfect **Sacrifice** for all of mankind.

All, throughout the ages of eternity, mankind will remember the heroic battle that Jesus shaped and won, to prove to humanity that God is just, and He could stand on legal grounds to justify the ungodly, because His only begotten Son had paid the price for every person, with His own blood.

When the first Adam sinned, his spirit died immediately. Just as God had told him **in the day** you eat of the fruit you will die. And so it was that Adam's spirit died to God and immediately it passed from life to death.

Now in reverse order when we believe in the Lord Jesus Christ as our Substitute our spirit passes from death to life. It is our spirit that is resurrected, justified, and made righteous.

But also, like the first Adam, his body and soul were not instantly changed. Remember Adam lived 930 years in his physical body before it died and returned to dust.

Now in a similar manner, when man accepts this gift of salvation, his spirit is immediately resurrected, becomes alive to God, and is free of the **penalty of sin**. Similarly, it will also take more time for man's body and soul to be sanctified and changed, to be freed from the **power and presence of sin**. Man's body will be freed from the presence of sin, but not until the rapture. This is very important to understand. In the case of both the first and the last Adam the effect of sin and salvation happened in the spiritual realm first.

The Holy Spirit Dwells in Us

So now man's spirit is justified and made righteous before God. As a result, there is another very significant change in man's being. Just as Jesus promised the Holy Spirit comes to dwell in man's spirit.

> *The Holy Spirit dwells in our spirit*

Just prior to Jesus going to the cross He is speaking to His disciples, and He is telling them that He must be crucified, and He must leave so that He can send the Holy Spirit.

*John 14:16 (NKJV) ¹⁶ And I will pray the Father, and He will **give you another Helper,** that He may abide with you forever—*

*John 14:17 (NKJV) ¹⁷ the Spirit of truth, whom the world cannot receive, because it neither sees Him nor knows Him; but you know Him, for **He dwells with you and will be in you.***

The Father, Son, and Holy Spirit are holy. They cannot and will not dwell with sin. We should be forever thankful for their holiness because we can have confidence He will not change.

The only reason the Holy Spirit can dwell in our spirit is because our spirit is a new creation in Christ Jesus. Our spirit is pure and holy and without sin. Our spirit is sealed, separated from the world and sin cannot enter it, even though our flesh still has a sin nature.

Why did Jesus send the Holy Spirit to dwell in us? Jesus told us that as He was leaving this earth, He would send us the Holy Spirit to be our Helper. It is so incredible that God lives inside of us to help us live our life properly while we are in this world. We can talk to Him and listen to Him 24/7. What a tremendous gift.

The challenge is that many people don't understand is that their flesh still has a sin-nature. Our body and soul (flesh) are used to sitting on the throne of our being, in other words, they want to continue being in charge. Prior to being born-again that is all you have known. Your flesh is not used to listening and obeying your spirit.

Your "will" is part of your soul; it's the part that makes decisions in your being and it needs to be sanctified and allow your spirit to sit on the throne of your being. Our spirit is strong but gentle and the Holy Spirit is most certainly strong, and He also is gentle. Neither are loud, boisterous, and boldly demanding. On the other hand, the sinful nature of our body and selfish self of our soul can be very loud and demanding. Our soul must determine which voices to obey.

Consequently, we frequently see born-again individuals struggling with sin. For example, if a person was an alcoholic before being born again, that person will likely still be an alcoholic after accepting Jesus as their Savior because their body still craves the alcohol, and their soul has only known the information it has received through their bodies and their previously dead spirit. Your soul is still selfish. God knew and understood this, so He provided a means to be sanctified.

Therefore, this person doesn't have to remain as an alcoholic, because the born-again person does have the power of the Holy Spirit in them, and they have the authority over alcohol.

As our spirit develops or strengthens, it should assume its position as ruler of our being. This can happen immediately if a person allows his spirit to be on the throne of his being, or it can be a process that takes time. The decision is made in our soul (in our "will"). Our soul should get its guidance from our spirit, and our soul should take charge over our bodies. This is an ongoing process that will continue through spiritual nourishment and renewing of our mind.

Our Authority Is Restored

> *Colossians 1:13 (NKJV)* [13] *He has delivered us from the power of darkness and conveyed us into the kingdom of the Son of His love,*

This is a very key scripture. In His death, burial, and resurrection Jesus took back all authority that Satan usurped from Adam. And when we are born-again, He delivers us from the power of darkness and transfers us into His kingdom. That means He has given us power over the works of the devil. There is no sin in God's kingdom and that is where He has invited us to live. While we are living in our current bodies, we are in this world and exposed to sin, but our born-again spirit is exempt from sin. Sin has absolutely no power or authority in our newly created spirit. Jesus already won that battle for us. Now we as born-again believers need to learn how to be led by the Spirit.

In this next section let's look a little closer at more effects from the cross. Jesus died for our sins, not only mine but every other person that has been, or is, or will be here tomorrow. That is a lot of sins.

It is a simple choice to trust Him as our Lord and Savior and to believe in Jesus' death, burial, and resurrection and then we have access to be set free from sin. That means He came to save us from eternal death. Jesus paid a significant price with His life to give us this offer of life for eternity with Him. When we believe in Him and confess Jesus as Lord of our life, we are born-again, that is, we are born of the Spirit and our spirit is born again. This is because Jesus took our sin and the judgement that comes with it on Himself. Our spirit becomes a new creation that is without sin.

Sanctification

As we begin to review the process of sanctification it may be helpful to recall the purpose of the spirit, soul, and body. Our spirit is God conscious, our soul is self-conscious, and our body is worldly conscious. Since sanctification is the process for salvation in our soul the focus of this section will be on self.

The last section was focused on justification and spirit. When we confessed and believed in Jesus through grace by faith our **spirit was justified**, and we received His righteousness. It was a one-time experience.

Jesus died once, He was judged once, and He was resurrected once. He did it right the first time and He doesn't need to do it again.

Since justification was a one-time experience for Jesus, similarly, we don't need to repeat the process of justification over and over again. Just as Jesus completed the process once, our spirit is justified in faith, and it is also a one-time experience. The penalty for sin is death. Jesus died for us as a Substitute to pay the penalty for our sin. Therefore, it is because we have faith that He died for our sins, and He paid the **penalty for our sins** so that our spirit is justified, and we became a new creation in Christ.

Sanctification on the other hand is how we are saved from the **power of sin**. Sanctification is not a one-time experience, it is a lifelong, continual process. We will need to look deeper into the Bible to understand the daily processes required to be sanctified and successfully walk through the challenges of living victoriously in Christ, in a sinful world.

To understand sanctification of the soul we should look at where sin resides in our being and what is its source of power. Secondarily we need to understand the basic operation process of our soul.

Where Is Sin Nature and Its Power?

It is important to establish a foundation but not get too caught up with semantics. Which comes first? The chicken or the egg?

Similarly, we can ask – where did sin enter into Adam? We could say that he ate the forbidden fruit in his body and God told him that when he ate the fruit he would die. So, the first argument is that sin entered through his body when he ate the fruit.

However, Adam had to think about and consider what and why he wanted to eat the fruit and then decide with his will that he would eat the fruit. So, the second argument is that because he thought about it in his mind, mixed it in with his emotions, and then decided in his "will" to eat it, then we can conclude sin entered through his soul.

Let's look at a few scriptures about the location of sin.

> *Romans 6:6 (NKJV) ⁶ knowing this, that our old man was crucified with Him, that the **body of sin** might be done away with, that we should no longer be slaves of sin.*

> *Colossians 2:11 (NKJV) ¹¹ In Him you were also circumcised with the circumcision made without hands, by putting off the **body of the sins** of the flesh, by the circumcision of Christ,*

> *Romans 6:12 (NKJV) ¹² Therefore do not let **sin reign in your mortal body**, that you should obey it in its lusts.*

We can conclude from these scriptures that sin resides in the body. But if we go back to our discussions in Genesis 2:7 there is no power in the body on its own. The body was not animated, or we could say it didn't come alive until the Spirit of God breathed life into Adam and his soul operated his body. His soul told his body to breathe, his soul told his heart to pump blood and so on. So, the body needs the soul, and the soul needs the body to function on the earth. Likewise, the body can't sin without the assistance of the soul. But the soul can't express sin without the body.

As you recall, when Adam sinned, he chose to be independent from God and his spirit died to God immediately. Therefore, because Adam's spirit was no longer on the throne of his being, and the fruit he ate was intended to open his soul to have access to knowledge of good and evil his soul was leading his way. This was what we can refer to as the formation of the first fleshly man.

What is the Flesh?

Flesh can have different meanings. For example, it can be used to describe the soft tissue part of our body. The part of our body that doesn't have bone or organs. This can describe the flesh of mankind or other creatures on earth.

> *1 John 4:2 (NKJV) ² By this you know the Spirit of God: Every spirit that confesses that **Jesus Christ has come in the flesh** is of God,*

As we can see in this scripture flesh can also be used to describe earthly beings in a general sense. It was critical that Jesus came to earth in flesh and blood because it is the legal method of entry into this world. So, Jesus came to earth in the flesh, but He did not have a sin nature.

However, the Bible and more particularly the New Testament commonly refers to flesh as the part of man that sins. Olive Tree Enhanced Strong's Dictionary describes flesh this way; the flesh, denotes mere human nature, the earthly nature of man **apart from divine influence**, and therefore prone to sin and opposed to God.

In using these definitions, we can also say, flesh would incorporate the body and the soul, and it is where sin operates in man. We can also say that the body and soul created an alliance that we refer to as the flesh. Below is a simple and clear description in scripture that will help us to easily identify works of the flesh.

> *Galatians 5:19-21 (NKJV) Now the **works of the flesh are evident,** which are: adultery, fornication, uncleanness, lewdness, ²⁰ idolatry, sorcery, hatred, contentions, jealousies, outbursts of wrath, selfish ambitions, dissensions, heresies, ²¹ envy, murders, drunkenness, revelries, and the like; of*

which I tell you beforehand, just as I also told you in time past, that those who practice such things will not inherit the kingdom of God.

Obviously, this is not a complete compilation of all sins, it is simply a list of some examples of the works of the flesh.

Romans 7:18 (NKJV) [18] *For I know that in me (that is, in my flesh)* **nothing good dwells;** *for to will is present with me, but how to perform what is good I do not find.*

The Apostle Paul makes this even more clear by saying *"in my flesh, nothing good dwells."* To capture and understand this statement we should go back to the definition used above; the flesh, denotes mere human nature, the earthly nature of man **apart from divine influence**, and therefore prone to sin and opposed to God. In other words, the Apostle Paul was saying that it is critical to understand the source of a thing in order to determine its value to your being.

In the garden of Edan, Adam could have eaten from the tree of life which would have provided him eternal life with God. It was this tree that represented God and life. It required Adam to be dependent on God for his eternal life.

Adam's other option was to eat fruit from the tree of knowledge of good and evil. It represented death which is from Satan. This tree provided **knowledge of good and evil,** and the source of that knowledge would come from or flow through his soul, not his spirit. This knowledge did not represent God. It represented independence from God.

When we choose to be born-again, we are choosing eternal life with God, which comes from God into our being through our spirit. Conversely, knowledge of good and evil comes from our soul which can incorporate our flesh.

Basic Operations of the Soul

As discussed, we receive life from God. Our relationship with Him begins in our spirit – in fact if we are born-again, He dwells in our spirit. In our spirit we are God Conscious. In our body we have a relationship with the world, and we are worldly conscious. We communicate with the world through our five senses. Unfortunately, because of Adam's sin, and the presence of Satan and his minions the world has been infiltrated with sin.

It is in our soul that we receive the inputs from our spirit and inputs from our body. Our soul can process all these inputs and our soul can even develop its own inputs.

Our soul, which is invisible and immortal, primarily consists of our mind, will, and emotions; or we could say it is where we think, feel, and choose.

- In our mind we use our intellect to process information. We can reason back and forth to analyze information. Note that this is not the brain. The brain is part of the body.

- In our analysis we can add flavor, or color to the information by adding emotion into the analysis process. When we add emotion, we can change our view of information significantly. We can easily make something that is bad look good or something that is good to look bad.

- Imagination is also part of our soul. If we add some imagination to the reasoning or analysis process, we can further modify the "knowledge of good or evil" significantly.

Another way to consider the "information we are processing" is to consider it as the "thoughts we are processing".

In other words, we obtain thoughts from various sources and process them through our mind, will, and emotions. When we receive a thought, we analyze it to determine what we want to do with that thought. We determine if we want to dwell on that thought, and if we decide that we do want to dwell on that thought, and which emotions do we want to add to our consideration of that thought. God is the only one besides us that sees and knows our thoughts. Nobody else knows our thoughts unless we reveal them to others. That includes the devil and evil spirits.

This whole process can be referred to as our self-consciousness. We could say the soul is our central processing station. It is where we become aware of all activities and thoughts in our being or in our life. The Bible has much to say about thoughts and how to manage thoughts and what are the effects of the way we process our thoughts.

Our soul is all about self. Our soul makes us aware of our spirit, soul, and body as well as all the thoughts that come from our spirit, soul, and body.

Jesus was our perfect example of how we should manage our soul. He showed us how to be selfless and not selfish. Most importantly He showed us how to become dependent on God and not independent from God.

Thoughts are how we establish the things we believe in. The things we that believe, come from, and are established from the things that we think. And we know that the things we believe determine our future. So, managing our thoughts properly is vitally important to our life.

Let's add another consideration, that as we dwell on thoughts then thoughts can become intentions. Then intentions drop down into our heart. Jesus speaks of this process quite a bit. He talks about as a man lust after a woman he has committed adultery in his heart. He spoke anger and committing murder in the same manner. Jesus is simply stating the importance of managing thoughts properly because they can lead to sin. But we use the same process of managing our thoughts when we receive salvation.

> *Romans 10:8-10 (NKJV) But what does it say? "The word is near you, in your mouth and in your heart" (that is, the word of faith which we preach): ⁹ that if you confess with your mouth the Lord Jesus and believe in your heart that God has raised Him from the dead, you will be saved. ¹⁰ For with the heart one believes unto righteousness, and with the mouth confession is made unto salvation.*

This scripture says the word is near you. That is an indication the thought is in your soul, and you are dwelling on Jesus with your intellect and emotions. In your "will" you are committing to Him and it becomes an intention as the thought drops into your heart. For with the heart, one believes unto righteousness. This is the process we discussed for faith. Then, out of the abundance of your heart your mouth speaks.

Sanctification is Dying to Flesh and Walking in the Spirit

We have already learned the penalty for sin is death. Our spirit is born-again, but we still have a sin nature.

We learned in Romans 7:18 "nothing good dwells in the flesh." Sin nature is part of our flesh and mankind can't control it on his own. Therefore, Jesus died for us. He was crucified in the flesh. We can't tame the flesh, if we could tame the flesh then Jesus would not have had to die on the cross.

> *Galatians 5:24-25 (NLT) Those who belong to Christ Jesus have nailed the passions and desires of their **sinful nature** to his cross and crucified them there. ²⁵ Since we are living*

by the Spirit, let us follow the Spirit's leading in every part of our lives.

The NLT translation uses the term **sinful nature** while the NKJV translation uses the term **flesh.** As we discussed, both terms represent the sinful part of man. This scripture is telling us that those of us that are in Christ, meaning those of us that are born-again, have already nailed those passions and desires of our flesh to **His** cross. We don't have to be physically nailed to a cross because Jesus already did it for us. This is one of the many benefits of our salvation.

Our first focus then should be to identify with the death of Jesus and die to our flesh. Similar, but opposite to our previous position when our spirit was dead to God. Now as we are born-again, we are alive to Him in our spirit and dead to our flesh. This is spiritual warfare. Our spirit is in opposition to our flesh.

> *Romans 6:6 (NKJV) ⁶ knowing this, that our **old man** was crucified with Him, that the **body of sin** might be done away with, that we should no longer be slaves of **sin.***

Let's consider three key terms in this scripture.

1. "old man"

2. "body of sin"

3. "sin" (singular in number)

These three terms are vastly different in their nature and all three play unique roles in the act of sinning and salvation.

1. The *"old man"* is referring to the status of man after Adam's sin and judgement. More specifically it is another reference to man's flesh which is incorporating our soul. To effectively deal with the sin problem the **"old man" was crucified with Jesus.**

2. The" *body of sin*" we have already explained that this is our sin nature and it's referring to sin being in man's body. This is incorporated in our flesh. As we are crucified and die to our flesh, we are no longer slaves to sin.

3. "*Sin*" is used here in singular form implying that it wants to be king of our being. It wants you to think about sin all the time. Sins desire is to rule over each one of us as slaves to it and it has the capacity to do so if we allow it.

In the sanctification process we need to consider all three of these three key terms referencing our flesh. And we can identify with the fact that Jesus Christ was crucified in the flesh on our behalf. The benefit is the same as if we were crucified.

> *Colossians 3:5 (NLT)* [5] ***So put to death the sinful, earthly things lurking within you.*** *Have nothing to do with sexual immorality, impurity, lust, and evil desires. Don't be greedy, for a greedy person is an idolater, worshiping the things of this world.*

In summary, as this scripture states – "*put to death the sinful earthly things…*" These things must die so that we can live.

Walking in the Spirit

> *Romans 8:13-17 (NKJV) For if you live according to the flesh you will die; but if by the Spirit you put to death the deeds of the body, you will live.* [14] *For as many as are led by the Spirit of God, these are sons of God.* [15] *For you did not receive the spirit of bondage again to fear, but you received the Spirit of adoption by whom we cry out, "Abba, Father."* [16] *The Spirit Himself bears witness with our spirit that we are children of God,* [17] *and if children, then heirs—heirs of*

God and joint heirs with Christ, if indeed we suffer with Him, that we may also be glorified together.

This scripture makes it clear – we can choose to live according to our flesh or according to our spirit. If we live according to our flesh, we will die. If we live according to the Spirit, then we will put to death the deeds of the body and we will live.

Galatians 5:16-18 (NKJV) ¹⁶ I say then: Walk in the Spirit, and you shall not fulfill the lust of the flesh. ¹⁷ For the flesh lusts against the Spirit, and the Spirit against the flesh; and these are contrary to one another, so that you do not do the things that you wish. ¹⁸ But if you are led by the Spirit, you are not under the law.

So, how do we walk according to the spirit? We have already looked at the works of the flesh which bring darkness and death. Now let's look at the fruit of the Spirit that displays light and life.

Galatians 5:22-25 (NKJV) But the fruit of the Spirit is love, joy, peace, longsuffering, kindness, goodness, faithfulness, ²³ gentleness, self-control. Against such there is no law. ²⁴ And those who are Christ's have crucified the flesh with its passions and desires. ²⁵ If we live in the Spirit, let us also walk in the Spirit.

The fruit here is singular and it has nine different characteristics. Remember the Holy Spirit dwells in us because He is our Helper. That is what He wants to do. He is always with us to support us and guide us. But we do have to purpose to listen to Him. This is all part of our walk of faith.

*2 Peter 1:5-8 (NLT) In view of all this, make every effort to respond to God's promises. **Supplement your faith***

with a generous provision of moral excellence, and moral excellence with knowledge,[6] and knowledge with self-control, and self-control with patient endurance, and patient endurance with godliness,[7] and godliness with brotherly affection, and brotherly affection with love for everyone.
[8] The more you grow like this, the more productive and useful you will be in your knowledge of our Lord Jesus Christ.

Peter is giving us further instruction regarding walking in the Spirit. He is encouraging us to take some **supplements** to strengthen our faith and spiritual walk.

Colossians 3:1-2 (NLT) Since you have been raised to new life with Christ, set your sights on the realities of heaven, where Christ sits in the place of honor at God's right hand. [2] ***Think about the things of heaven, not the things of earth.***

We should be proposing to think about things of heaven. Our thoughts should be proactive towards the spiritual matters of God.

Spiritual Man or Carnal Man

Who are you a slave too? Who are you obedient too?

Romans 6:16-22 (NKJV) Do you not know that to whom you present yourselves slaves to obey, you are that one's slaves whom you obey, whether of sin leading to death, or of obedience leading to righteousness? [17] But God be thanked that though you were slaves of sin, yet you obeyed from the heart that form of doctrine to which you were delivered. [18] And having been set free from sin, you became slaves of righteousness. [19] I speak in human terms because of the weakness of your flesh. For just as you presented your members as slaves of uncleanness, and of lawlessness leading to more lawlessness, so now present your members as slaves of righteousness for holiness. [20] For when you were slaves of sin, you were free in regard to righteousness. [21] What fruit did you have then in the things of which you are now ashamed? For the end of those things is death. [22] But now having been set free from sin, and having become slaves of God, you have your fruit to holiness, and the end, everlasting life.

Are we slaves to sin or slaves to righteousness?

Romans 8:5-8 (NKJV) For those who live according to the flesh set their minds on the things of the flesh, but those who live according to the Spirit, the things of the Spirit. [6] For to be carnally minded is death, but to be spiritually minded is life and peace. [7] Because the carnal mind is enmity against God; for it is not subject to the law of God, nor indeed can be. [8] So then, those who are in the flesh cannot please God.

Paul is bringing more clarification – we can be carnally minded or spiritually minded.

*Romans 7:24-25 (NKJV) O wretched man that I am! Who will deliver me from this body of death? [25] I thank God—through Jesus Christ our Lord! So then, with **the mind** I myself serve the law of God, but with **the flesh** the law of sin.*

Now here we have a distinction of the mind or the flesh. This is the spiritual man vs the carnal man.

> *Ephesians 4:30 (NLT) And do not bring sorrow to God's Holy Spirit by the way you live. Remember, he has identified you as his own, guaranteeing that you will be saved on the day of redemption.*

Every believer knows that Jesus died on the cross for us. But there is much more to His death than just dying. To be the perfect sacrifice for our sins He proposed to identify with us and our sins. To experience the effect of our sins He had to experience the impact of sin the way that we experience the effect of our sins. To suffer for us. To take on our full judgement for all our sins. Let's look at how Jesus suffered in His spirit, soul, and body.

Now let's recognize that in the first phase of our salvation it is our spirit that is regenerated. There is no immediate change in our soul and body, or what we could refer to as the alliance that we call our flesh. In the next section (Glorification) we will learn that we will get a new body that is without sin in the resurrection. But first let's look at how to sanctify ourselves (souls) each day while living in this world.

> *Ephesians 4:21-24 (NLT) Since you have heard about Jesus and have learned the truth that comes from him,²² throw off your old sinful nature and your former way of life, which is corrupted by lust and deception. ²³ Instead, let the Spirit renew your thoughts and attitudes. ²⁴ Put on your new nature, created to be like God—truly righteous and holy*

We can see in these last three chapters of Ephesians a guide to successful daily living principles. We can see the desires of God for us. These principles are not an extension of the law but rather a practical guide to living in the Spirit and how to be led by the Spirit of God who dwells in us. We can see that not only in the book of Ephesians, but throughout the Bible how we get saved and how to walk out our salvation. There are practical tools to manage and renew our thoughts and attitudes as we put on our new nature in Christ.

Glorification

Glorification is God's final removal of the **presence of sin** from the life of the saints so that they stand complete and faultless before Him in glory throughout eternity. By now you understand our current body incorporates a sin nature. At the resurrection we will get a new glorified body that is without sin.

Let's begin this section with a brief review and description of our current body. As we have discussed, God created the first Adam from elements of the earth such as; water, air (gasses) and multiple minerals from the ground. God combined these elements in various mixtures and in such a manner as to form our various organs, bones, flesh, and blood.

Then God assembled all these members to form them into the shape of our body, but there was no life in our body until God breathed the breath of life into Adam's nostrils. At that point in time, his body came to life and Adam's body became animated. This is our natural or physical body. God designed man's body to be immortal, but because Adam sinned, he was judged, condemned and sentenced to death.

Consequently, we now have sin as part of our physical nature or DNA and as a result, just like Adam, our body is mortal. Meaning that our physical body will die and return to dust because it is infected with sin.

But the Bible tells us that in the last phase or part of our salvation, we will get a new glorified body at the time of our resurrection. This new body will be free from sin, and it will be immortal. Let's look at some details about this new body and when we will get this new body.

Two Resurrections

We have already discussed that God established for mankind two births and two deaths. Now we will discuss the two resurrections. As we also learned everyone born into this world will die the first death, which is the physical consequence of sin. The only exclusion is those that are alive in the earth at the time of the rapture. Now let's look at the two resurrections.

> *John 5:28-29 (NKJV) ²⁸ Do not marvel at this; for the hour is coming in which all who are in the graves will hear His voice ²⁹ and come forth—those who have done good, to the* **resurrection of life***, and those who have done evil, to the* **resurrection of condemnation***.*

This scripture is simply saying that everyone born in the world will be resurrected. The only questions are when will you be resurrected, and where will you be resurrected to? This scripture clearly tells us there are two resurrections: the resurrection of life and the resurrection of condemnation.

First Resurrection

Jesus is the first fruits of the first resurrection.

> *1 Corinthians 15:20-22 (NKJV) But now Christ is risen from the dead, and has become the firstfruits of those who have fallen asleep. ²¹ For since by man came death, by Man also came the resurrection of the dead. ²² For as in Adam all die, even so in Christ all shall be made alive.*

First fruits means that Jesus was the first to be risen from the dead. He was the example or the first of mankind to be fully resurrected from the dead. In a different but similar manner the first Adam was the first fruits for sin and death. Just as Adam was the pattern for sin and death now Jesus is the pattern for righteousness and life.

Let's expand on this statement that Christ became the first fruits. In the Old Testament, the first crops at the beginning of harvest season were to be dedicated to God, Exod. 23:19, Deut. 26:2. This applied to grains and produce or firstborn animals. It was making a statement of appreciation and of gratitude to God with hopeful expectations of a good overall harvest. Christ's resurrection is the first of a great harvest of God's people who will be resurrected.

You might say, but there were others that were raised from the dead before Jesus was resurrected. How can Jesus be called first fruits? That is a good question, and you would be partially correct, but..... These previous examples of people coming back to life would include the widow's son in Luke 7:11, Lazarus in John 11:38, the 12-year-old girl in Mark 5:41 and others. While these are all great miracles, there are at least three significant differences between the miracles of these people that were raised from the dead, and the resurrection of Jesus.

1. The first difference is that all these people in the other examples eventually, physically died again. In other words, they were raised from the dead in their mortal bodies, and they would all die again and return to dust. Jesus was the first man to die and come back to life for eternity (in a new immortal body).

2. Their spirit came back with their body, but it was still dead to God. Jesus came back alive to God in His spirit.

3. In all these examples each person raised from the dead still had a sin nature, Jesus did not.

We have already discussed the legal authority for the resurrection of Jesus and how believers are now included because of what Jesus did for us on the cross. Jesus established and opened the door for all His followers (believers) to be part of the first resurrection.

> *1 Corinthians 15:23-24 (NKJV) But each one in his own order: Christ the firstfruits, afterward those who are Christ's at His coming. ²⁴ Then comes the end, when He delivers the kingdom to God the Father, when He puts an end to all rule and all authority and power.*

There are multiple resurrection groups that will experience the first resurrection and at different times. Here is a listing of the groups.

1. Jesus Christ the firstfruits.

2. The next group after Jesus will be the Church, the bride of Christ.

    > *1 Thessalonians 4:16-17 (NKJV) ⁶ For the Lord Himself will descend from heaven with a shout, with the voice of an archangel, and with the trumpet of God. And the dead in Christ will rise first. ¹⁷ Then we who are alive and remain shall be caught up together with them in the clouds to meet the Lord in the air. And thus we shall always be with the Lord.*

    The Church will essentially include all born-again believers from the day of Pentecost until the time of the rapture. This will take place before the tribulation period begins as we are further preparing for the wedding. The Church here is identified as those that have already experienced the first death and their bodies have begun or completed the decaying process of returning to dust and those believers that are still alive on earth. The Bible doesn't give us details about how Christ collects the dust and remaining bodies. It just tells us we will be caught up together and meet up with the Lord and be with Him forever more.

3. Then during the tribulation period, the next group to be resurrected, will be the two witnesses in Revelation 11:11.

4. At the end of the tribulation period, those that are saved during the tribulation period in Revelation 20:4, the rest of the dead which would include Old Testament saints, and all of Israel that is still alive will be resurrected.

All these groups are part of the first resurrection.

Second Resurrection

The second resurrection is very simple. You would be wise to get your reservations in now for the first call in the first resurrection, because you really don't want to wait and be invited to this gathering, the second resurrection, Revelation 20:12,13. This is the gathering for the great white throne judgement.

It takes place at the end of the millennial period, and it includes all the non-believers. Death and Hades will also be at this gathering. Anyone whose name is not found in the book of life will experience the second death which happens at the great white throne of judgement, and they will be sentenced to spend eternity in the Lake of Fire or Hell.

Description of Our New Body

What is this new body like? How is it different from our current body? We don't know everything about our new body, but we do have quite a bit of information. Let's start with a close look at 1 Corinthians chapter 15:35. Paul starts by saying we will sow our current body in the soil similar to wheat or some other grain and it won't come alive until it first dies. Just like the grain you sow the seed that is dead, you don't sow the body that it will be, rather as it grows God will give it a body as He pleases and to each seed its own body.

The verses go on and describe some of the direct comparisons of our current body that is sown, and the new body God gives us.

- earthly vs. heavenly (verse 40)
- corruption vs. incorruption (verse 42)
- dishonorable vs. glorified (verse 43)
- subject to weakness vs. raised in power (verse 43)
- natural vs. spiritual (verse 44)
- image of the man of the dust vs. image of the heavenly Man (verse 49)
- mortal vs. immortal (verse 53)

Let's look at what the disciple saw when Jesus showed His resurrected body.

> *Luke 24:39 (NKJV) [39] Behold My hands and My feet, that it is I Myself. Handle Me and see, for a spirit does not have flesh and bones as you see I have.*

Jesus wanted them to know He wasn't a ghost.

Jesus is showing His disciples that He is real. They can touch and feel His body, even though His resurrected body is a spiritual body just like ours will be. But Jesus recognized they still had some doubts.

> *Luke 24:40-43 (NKJV) When He had said this, He showed them His hands and His feet. [41] But while they still did not believe for joy, and marveled, He said to them, "Have you any food here?" [42] So they gave Him a piece of a broiled fish and some honeycomb. [43] And He took it and ate in their presence.*

So, to further validate Jesus eats some food which indicates that He can chew, swallow and digest. Jesus showed them that He could eat, but most likely our new glorified bodies won't require that we eat because our nutrition will come directly from God.

> *John 20:19 (NKJV)* [19] *Then, the same day at evening, being the first day of the week, when the doors were shut where the disciples were assembled, for fear of the Jews, Jesus came and stood in the midst, and said to them, "Peace be with you."*

The disciples were in fear of the Jews and stayed locked up in the room. Jesus walked through the walls in His glorified body.

His glorified body was not restricted from gravity. We know this because He ascended into heaven.

Receiving our glorified body is the final step in our salvation process. However, it is important to remember that we are not left helpless until that time. We still have victory in our current body. We have already discussed the authority Jesus provided to us now on this earth.

In summary, God created mankind in perfection. As a result of the first Adam's sin, all of mankind has been infected with sin and the result of that sin is eternal death which is separation from God for eternity. In other words our complete salvation is a process, and we will return to the status of perfection into eternity.

Personal Comments

As mentioned in the introduction, I was led to compile all the notes from my studies of spirit, soul, and body into the form of a book. My original plan was to focus on the details of the form, features, and functions of the spirit, soul, and body but to my surprise, as I was writing, I was led to focus more on the history and future of man's spirit, soul, and body. It is my plan to write more books on this topic that will apply to practical understanding and application of mankind's spirit, soul, and body.

As we reflect on the overall perspective of mankind, we can see several key elements in God's Word (the Bible) that can help us to understand our purpose in life, our destination for eternity, and most importantly God's love for us. In summary we can see the following statements.

- God is perfection. He is truth, love, and He is holy.
- God created man in perfection. We were made in His image and likeness.
- Mankind turned away from God to seek his independence from God.
- In mankind's rebellion (seeking his independence from God), he was destined to eternity without God and to spend eternity in hell.
- The Bible is the love story of how God sent His only Son to die on the cross for our sins, so that we could be saved and spend eternity with Him.

- If we choose to believe in Him as our substitute for death and as our Savior, we can experience the zoe life He promised us both here on earth and into eternity.

As we look at the world in which we live, we can see the effects of sin everywhere. Many people all around us are hurt and broken, filled with fear, seemingly without hope. There is tremendous abuse of drugs, both legal and illegal, having a profound negative impact on people. Mental confusion and sickness are growing out of control. The effects of perversion in many forms are causing confusion and mental anguish. Bitterness and hatred are stirring up divisions of people everywhere causing arguments, battles, and even wars between individuals, families, and nations. People's ability to distinguish right from wrong is significantly impaired. Consequently sickness and disease are flourishing throughout our society.

My hope and prayer is that you recognize the status of the world in which we live and that you accept Jesus as your Lord and Savior. In doing so you can have freedom from sin in this world. God said we can overcome by the blood of the Lamb and the word of our testimony. You can obtain this freedom right now by praying this prayer below.

Lord Jesus, I recognize that I am a sinner and I repent of every sin and work of darkness in my life. I accept you now Jesus, as my personal Lord and Savior. I accept the great exchange of Your nature for my old nature; of Your love for my hatred, bitterness, envy, and strife; of Your wisdom and ability for my natural ability; of Your prosperity in spirit, soul, and body for my poverty; of "heaven on earth" now as opposed to "hell on earth" where, without You, I have no authority to overcome the temptations and attacks of the devil.

Thank You Lord Jesus for empowering me with Your Spirit and equipping me to live an overcoming life of victory here on earth now.

If you prayed this prayer and believe it in your heart, then you are born again. Your spirit is a new creation, and you have eternal life with Jesus. As you have read in this book, you will continue walking out your sanctification process.

www.ingramcontent.com/pod-product-compliance
Lightning Source LLC
Chambersburg PA
CBHW062126020426
42335CB00013B/1114